MINDFUL MAMA
Happy Baby

**Over 60 calming techniques and creative
activities for babies and toddlers**

Maja Pitamic & Susannah Marriott

Contents

Chapter 5 ARTS AND CRAFTS 80

Chapter 6 MINDFUL GAMES AND MOVEMENT 96

Chapter 7 LANGUAGE AND STORIES 118

Chapter 8 OUT AND ABOUT 134

Templates 156

Index 160

Introduction by Susannah Marriott

Life turns upside down after the birth of a child. Everything we thought of as stable or fixed is up in the air: where and when we sleep, how we organise the home, our behaviour with partner, friends and family, our status in the world. So what better time to rethink routines and relationships, and seek a life that is more considered, calm and compassionate – or mindful?

Parents have an advantage in living mindfully – the cry of a baby is engineered to make us focus on that one need in the here and now. Mindful living teaches us to be aware that life is ever-changing: parents have a physical appreciation of time passing as a child grows and we rethink our expectations with each new stage.

This book is packed with easy mindful exercises to calm the whirlwind of thoughts and emotions and bring a little peace and perspective. There are mindful games to play, alongside activities to stimulate the senses, crafts projects to encourage creativity, and movement games that boost co-ordination. There are fun ways to get out and explore the world of nature through the seasons. And for quieter moments there are massages, yoga sequences and wind-down activities.

Playing with a child with awareness daily is the most mindful thing we can do as parents. It shows children we are available and passes on the self-acceptance that comes from engaging fully with an activity. As children reveal their personalities and unique ways of doing things so we learn from them, our relationships become richer and children feel truly loved. That positivity influences every part of development, physical, mental and emotional, and extends into every part of family life, building confident, happy children and kind, compassionate parents.

Development through play
by Maja Pitamic

As adults we often underestimate the value that play has in developing children both mentally and physically. Play is your child's way of engaging and making sense of the world and cannot be overvalued. Take an activity like role play. This may appear to be a very simple activity, yet within it young children can learn the practical life skills of dressing, setting the table and how to co-operate and share with others.

For adults the sense of sight is the dominant sense, but for very young children all their senses are heightened. A child's senses are their natural teaching tools for exploring their world. The games and activities contained in this book engage all the senses to develop your child's co-ordination, concentration and life skills. They will also help to relieve your child's sense of frustration, which is a key characteristic of this age group. Your child will be engaged both mentally and physically to gain a sense of independence and self-worth.

What is mindful parenting?

Put simply, being a mindful parent is just being more aware of life as it happens – noticing your thoughts, emotions and reactions, and choosing to act on them in a way that serves you best. This brings about calmness and a sense of well-being, giving you a break from the strong emotions and intense ups and downs of parenting. It also offers the perspective you need in order to keep recalibrating expectations and making good decisions as the months and years bring new parenting challenges.

As a parent, mindfulness is about paying full attention to a child when you interact, being aware of her as her own person while noticing your own emotions and expectations. It's as simple as holding the gaze of a newborn and doing nothing but revelling in that connection. There's no past or future; all that matters is what's happening between you now.

Why does mindfulness matter to parents? When we really connect to our children – by giving them our full attention when we're with them – we become calmer and more compassionate and children feel cherished. This sense of understanding creates a deep connection and a supportive home in which children feel accepted and loved. In these conditions children develop qualities that help them grow up happy and confident: empathy and kindness, honesty and co-operation, and the ability to reflect. Mindfulness is shown to help adults and children to sustain attention, regulate emotions, resist the effects of stress and become more resilient to life's knock-backs.

Early childhood is the time when children learn most quickly, and the way we nurture in the early years lays down lifelong neural pathways that influence how children understand the world and value themselves. Engaging with children in the way they naturally learn – through play – allows us to relive the carefree spontaneity of our own childhoods. Playing with children, we see the world afresh through the eyes of a child; this is mindful parenting.

How to use this book

This book provides mindfulness and play activities for you and your child, and is suitable for children from birth to three years. Each chapter contains activities aimed at a specific age group, and the first chapter includes mindfulness meditations, visualisations and movement exercises to help you adjust to your new role as a parent. The activities in subsequent chapters are based on Montessori principles of learning through experience. Maria Montessori believed that children flourish and grow in self-esteem within a child-centred environment where they are respected and listened to.

■ All the activities are suitable for boys and girls. To avoid repetition, the use of 'she' and 'he' is alternated in the chapters.

■ Each chapter opens with a timeline that marks key milestones in your child's development and offers notes on mindfulness. The timelines are a rough guide only; children develop at their own pace and some grasp new skills faster than others.

■ Check your environment. Make sure you and your child can do the activity in comfort and safety.

■ Ensure your child can see the activity clearly. Sit your child to the left of you (your right, if she is left-handed). Aim to work with your right hand (left hand for left-handed children).

■ Prepare in advance. There is no point suggesting an activity to a child only to discover you lack the materials.

■ Be clear in your mind what the aim of the activity is before you start; read through the text first.

■ Try not to be negative. If you or your child are unable to do the activity correctly, make a mental note to try it again at a later date.

■ If your child abuses any materials in the activity, remove the activity immediately so she understands that her behaviour is unacceptable. Introduce the activity at a later date.

■ While structure is necessary, be prepared to be flexible and don't worry if things don't always go to plan; play may lead you down unexpected paths of discovery and that's when things get exciting.

A new world

Congratulations – you are a parent! You're probably feeling slightly bewildered and incredibly tired, but keen to get to know your beautiful new baby. This chapter contains mindful ways to ease you and your family into parenthood and build a lifelong bond with your child. The most effective way to do this is to establish an environment in which your child can flourish and grow into a happy, confident person, and in which you can become a happy, confident parent. Mindfulness brings about a calm focus that helps you to build this supportive and positive environment, and it all starts with a loving cuddle.

Mindful timeline: 0–6 months

Your every interaction with your new baby is mindful; in the early weeks you will spend a good deal of time in deep eye contact with each other, when nothing else matters. When he's ready for a rest, your child will initiate it by looking away. When he cries, you have no option but to stop everything and focus on his needs. This close connection with your baby is vital for his brain development as well as for bonding. By the end of the first six months of life, your child will show you with his gestures, his smiles and the beginnings of speech that you are the most important person in his life.

Your baby understands a great deal in the early weeks of life: he recognises your voice and your smell, he is learning about the world through touch and establishing a bond with you through intense eye contact; he loves your face in particular.

The only plaything your baby needs right now is you – and the best times of day to engage are those short periods when your baby is quiet and alert. At around two months of age he may even reward you with his first smile.

Timeline

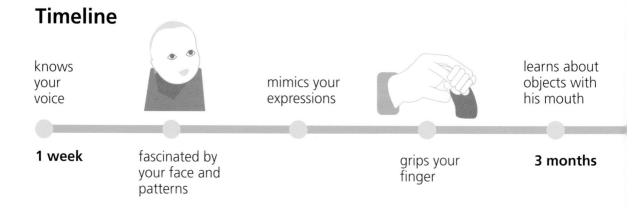

| knows your voice | | mimics your expressions | | learns about objects with his mouth |

1 week   fascinated by your face and patterns   grips your finger   **3 months**

A key method of communication for a young baby is crying. You'll soon learn to distinguish the different types of cries, and your baby feels comforted when you respond to his cries; this is the attachment process at work.

By three months, your child will start to notice and play with his hands. As his hand and eye co-ordination develops, he reaches out to try and bat at objects, then learns to grasp them, bringing things to his mouth – 'mouthing' is how he learns about the world. He'll clasp hands and play with his fingers and then his feet. He'll be able to hold his head and neck with more control, and push up on his hands to lift his head and chest when placed on his tummy, looking sideways and rolling over.

As the months pass, your child will become much more expressive, cooing, smiling and breaking into laughter; he'll make vowel sounds and start to initiate 'conversations' with you.

This chapter contains mindful activities such as a Change meditation to help you adjust to the new role of parent and a Welcome home babymoon to allow you to create a comforting space and savour quiet time with your baby.

better able to
control head
and neck

gets distracted
by surroundings

rolls
over

6 months

Mindful breathing

There's nothing more relaxing than holding a sleeping baby. Next time your newborn is asleep on your chest, try this relaxation technique that brings you mindfully in touch with your baby's breathing.

1 When your baby is asleep, close your eyes and tune in to his breathing, allowing it to erase other thoughts from your mind.

2 Notice how the breath expands your baby's abdomen and back – his whole body is breathing.

3 Now start to link your breath to his. Inhale for 2 or 3 of your baby's breaths; exhale for 2 or 3. Let your breath come naturally, noticing it cool at your nostrils as you inhale and warm as you exhale.

4 Feel your abdomen rising and your ribs expanding with each in-breath. Let your shoulders relax as you breathe out.

5 Start to extend your out-breath, so you inhale for 2 or 3 of your baby's breaths and exhale for 3 or 4.

6 Continue breathing in this way for 3 to 5 minutes, or until you fall asleep, too.

Refocusing visualisation

Life turns upside down when you become a parent. Priorities shift, relationships reform, your body does unexpected things; even time takes on a new meaning. This focusing visualisation re-centres you when life feels scattered.

1 Close your eyes and direct your gaze inwards. Take your thoughts to your toes, your fingers and the crown of your head. Notice any sensations you feel here.

2 Inhaling, imagine drawing energy up from your toes and into your pelvis. As you exhale let it gather and rest there. Repeat 2 or 3 times.

3 Now, inhale energy from the tips of your fingers up your arms, around your shoulders and down into your pelvis. Imagine it growing as you exhale. Repeat.

4 Draw energy down from the crown of your head as you inhale, allowing it to drop into your pelvis and expand as you exhale. Repeat.

5 Finally, visualise the energy centred in your pelvis as a pulsating ball of light. Feel its force and know it's there to support you.

Giving thanks

The birth of a child brings you into a new present where everything is up for renegotiation – and the possibilities for new starts are endless. It's a good time to be quiet and to express thanks, not just for the safe arrival of your precious bundle, but for the new person you are becoming as a parent.

1 Sit on a chair with your back well supported. Place your feet flat on the floor – on books or cushions if necessary. It's important that you feel well grounded and have a straight spine.

2 Rest the palms of your hands on your thighs and close your eyes. Start to focus on the flow of breath in and out of your body. This is always the simplest way to become more mindful.

3 When your breath has become slower and you feel more relaxed, bring your palms together in front of your chest. Rest your thumbs against your breast bone. Relax your elbows and draw your shoulder blades down your back, keeping your shoulders against the back of the chair. Press your palms together and broaden your chest.

4 Visualise your spine supporting your upper body. Feel it lengthen upwards and lift the sides of your waist. Appreciate how your spine supports the whole of the back of your body. In yoga, the back of the body represents the universe; you are supported by so many people. Give thanks to everyone who has helped you on the journey of parenthood so far.

5 Think about your palms meeting in front of your heart. In yoga this is seen as a physical gesture of union, representing the interconnectedness of all beings. Give thanks for that connection.

6 Finally, keeping your back straight, bow your chin forwards, honouring yourself and the compassion and love that reside within you.

Tip box ■ If you can't manage the full meditation, just bring your hands together and use this focus to direct your attention to your heart.

Welcome home babymoon

Bringing a life into the world ranks among the most momentous times of your life, so try to savour the moment as often as you can during the first weeks. When you get home with your baby, take some time just for yourselves so you can come together as a new family and anchor yourselves in your new world. In some cultures this resting-up, baby-centred time lasts for one cycle of the moon.

1 Create a cosy nest in one room – the bedroom is ideal. Put fresh linen on the bed, keep the lights dimmed and the space warm, and fill the room with flowers and cards. Focus your life here in this room with these incredible people for a few days.

2 Call in favours so that other people shop, cook and clean for you. This takes some organisation, but you'll find that people will want to help in a practical way at this special time if you allow them.

3 Encourage visitors to stay away; keep them satisfied with social-media updates. This is a time for you to look inwards, towards the heart of your new family.

You will need

- Fresh bed linen
- Flowers
- Deliveries of your favourite restorative food and drink
- Helpful friends, family and neighbours

Tip box ■ Don't feel guilty, and don't feel obliged to do anything other than be there for your baby. Mindfulness at this point is about savouring the serenity of the early days before a baby becomes more wakeful.

4 Adjust your time to baby time. Doze when he sleeps, talk to and stroke him when he wakes. Tune into his patterns of feeding, wakefulness, crying and quiet states of alertness.

5 Stare at this tiny being you know so intimately and yet have never seen; scrutinise that miraculous face before it becomes familiar, drinking in the intense eye contact newborns give.

6 Enjoy your new baby and the retreat for as long as you feel it is helping you to adjust, recuperate, gain in strength and prepare yourself to emerge as a new being: a parent.

Change meditation

New parenthood is about learning to ride immense upheaval. The secret of maintaining peace and equanimity during times of change lies in cultivating the flexibility to go with the flow and finding a way to let go of expectations.

1 When you feel overwhelmed by change, guide your thoughts to the matter at hand. This is the best way to halt a train of thought or distressing emotion. Attending to what you are doing right now makes you feel more in control of life as it is.

2 Lower your expectations. Aim to do just one thing a day – maybe as little as making a to-do list. Staying sane as a parent means starting to recalibrate what you can do in a day.

3 Stop anticipating: try not to worry about what will happen in an hour or a week's time, or how long the baby will sleep or feed. No two days will be the same for a while.

4 Focus on the big picture. It can bring relief to imagine your child at 5, 10 or 18 years old. This daily life is temporary, and it will keep changing.

Soothing to sleep

It can be hard to switch off despite the tiredness of the early days of parenthood. This meditation helps when you need to sleep – while baby is napping or after a night feed when he has dozed off and you're left wakeful.

1 Lie on your back, making sure you're warm. Close your eyes and place an eye pillow over your eyes if you have one. Start to feel the flow of your breath in and out. Feel how it expands your chest and ribs as you inhale. Notice how you sink into the support beneath you as you exhale.

2 Exhaling, relax the back of your head, your shoulder blades, pelvis and heels into the support beneath you. Feel your weight spreading and sinking downwards.

3 Release your jaw and imagine your forehead smoothing out. Let go of any tension in your belly. Visualise the space in your mouth becoming larger.

4 Scan your body from toes to head, and release any tension you notice. When thoughts arise, acknowledge them, sensing how they take the edge off your calm, then return to your focus. Either drift off now or enjoy the relaxed clarity for 10 minutes.

Swaddling your baby

Newborn babies can be disturbed by their own naturally jerky arm movements – the Moro or startle reflex – and some feel more secure and less restive if they are gently swaddled, so that they feel safely held. This technique can help parents adjust to the world of new babyhood, too, because it gives you the very welcome skill of being able to calm a fractious baby when you both feel overstimulated.

1 Place the cot sheet or thin blanket on the floor or bed in a diamond shape, then fold the top point under to create a straight edge along the top.

2 Lie your baby on his back on the sheet so that the top straight edge is level with the back of his neck.

3 Place your baby's left arm straight by his side and fold the left side of the sheet or blanket across his body, tucking the excess fabric beneath his back on his left side.

You will need

- A cotton baby cot sheet or thin blanket

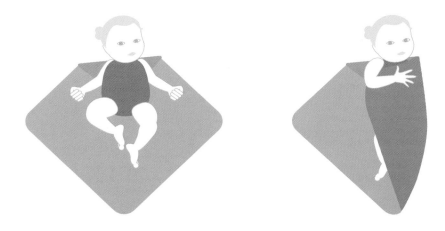

4 Place his right arm straight by his side, and fold the remaining side of the sheet or blanket across his body. Tuck the fabric beneath his back on the left side so he is snugly held. Don't make the wrap too tight; you should be able to slip a couple of fingers into the wrap.

5 Bunch the fabric around his legs and tuck it underneath him. Make sure there's enough room for his legs to move up and down, froggy style.

6 After about a month – and once he starts to roll over and kick off the blankets – your baby won't need swaddling to feel calm.

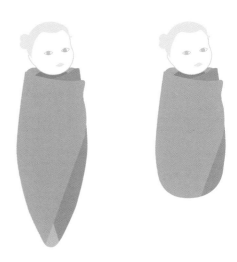

SAFETY POINTS !

Don't swaddle a baby who is hungry or needs a change.

It's important that your baby doesn't overheat, so make sure the swaddling fabric is thin; you may not need to use extra bedding.

Keep your baby's head uncovered.

Always place your baby on his back when swaddled.

Don't swaddle while feeding; babies need to use their hands while nursing.

Feeding focus

New breastfeeding mothers spend a good deal of time stranded on the sofa or in bed while feeding, which can make you feel rather immobile and stuck. This movement exercise refocuses the mind while bringing relief to tense shoulders.

1 Lie on the floor on your right side with your knees bent and your hips, legs and shoulders stacked. Make sure there's plenty of space behind you. Extend your arms along the ground in front of you, one on top of the other.

2 Inhaling, rotate the top arm slowly up behind your head, dragging your fingertips along the floor if you can. Keep rotating the arm behind you, drawing a semi-circle with your fingers and turning your head if that feels comfortable, until your left arm is stretched behind you and both arms are in a line.

3 Breathing out, bring the left arm back over your head, again dragging your fingertips along the floor, in a semi-circle shape until you reach the starting position, left arm stacked on the right, palms together.

4 Repeat the movement in steps 2 and 3 a few times. Glide your arm really slowly and focus your thoughts on your right shoulder, encouraging it to relax as you stretch the arm. When you find a stiff spot, move very slowly through the range of movement there, enjoying the stretch.

5 Rest for a few seconds in the starting position before rolling onto your back and over to your left side, knees bent and your hips, legs and arms stacked. Repeat the movement on the other side, extending your right arm up and behind your head, dragging your fingertips along the floor if you can, until both arms are outstretched in a line. Co-ordinate your breath with the movement and focus your thoughts on your left shoulder, feeling it loosen and relax. Repeat daily if you can.

Other activities to try

While feeding, relax your shoulders away from your ears as you exhale.

To encourage the let-down reflex when breastfeeding, imagine your milk as a copious fountain or never-ending thread.

Practise your pelvic-floor exercises as a mindful focus while feeding. At the end of an exhalation, pull up the muscles surrounding your anus and then those you use to stop yourself peeing. Hold for a moment. Release, then inhale. Repeat up to 12 times.

All will be well affirmation

If you feel lost or out of your depth as a new parent, the anchor of a single point of reference can be helpful in guiding you towards a more restful and controlled sense of awareness. This candle-gazing meditation is combined with an affirmation, a positive phrase to repeat to yourself, which works subliminally to restore a sense of calmness and control.

1. Place a lit candle on a low table and sit comfortably in front of it so that the flame is level with or slightly below your eyes. If it helps you feel more comfortable, sit on a cushion or some large books or yoga blocks, or sit with your back supported by a wall.

2. Close your eyes and focus your thoughts on yourself sitting in this room; try not to be distracted by other thoughts or by any feelings. Now open your eyes and look at the candle flame. Find the bright yellow central part of the flame that burns brightest and does not waver. Try not to blink as you fix your eyes on this point for a few seconds.

You will need

- A low table
- A candle

Tip box ▥ After some practise of this exercise, you should be able to look at the real candle flame for shorter amounts of time and hold the image in your mind for a longer period.

3 Now close your eyes and see the unwavering flame in your mind's eye. Nothing matters except that still point of the flame.

4 When the image fades or thoughts intrude, open your eyes and gaze at the flame once more; find that still point again. Feel your peripheral vision and intrusive thoughts fade away as you look at the flame. Try not to blink.

5 Close your eyes again and visualise the constant flame in your mind's eye. Repeat the phrase 'All will be well'. This phrase has the same constancy as the flame. Continue the candle-gazing exercise for up to 5 minutes before getting up carefully.

6 After you have finished the candle-gazing, repeat the phrase whenever you remember. You don't have to have faith in them for affirmations to be effective. Research suggests they may work by maintaining the ability to solve problems whilst under pressure.

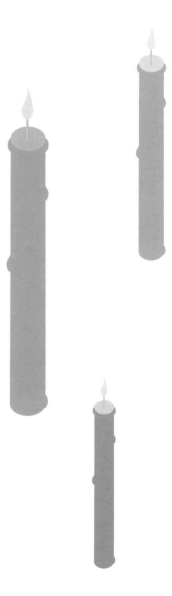

Getting to know you

Play is your child's way of engaging with and
making sense of the world, and this chapter is
packed with ways to play mindfully with your baby.
The activities will help you get to know your child
as she grows, discovering what excites, stimulates
and even frustrates her – and you! Best of all, as you
respond to your baby through these activities, you'll
be able to share your child's sense of accomplishment
when she masters a new skill or expresses herself
with more confidence. This boosts her sense of
independence and self-worth and shows you what a
great parent you are.

Mindful timeline: 6–12 months

In the months leading up to your child's first birthday, she really starts to express her personality and her affection for you. She'll be able to roll over, sit without support and crawl. If you hold her by the hands she may even take a few steps. She can pick up smaller objects and 'find' things you've hidden in a game. Emotionally, your baby can read your expressions and tone of voice, and express her own feelings back; she loves copying you. She'll also practise an early form of conversation, babbling – responding to her 'speech' and expressions is a key way to engage mindfully with your child.

Your child's understanding is such that she can respond to her name now and follow simple instructions. You'll be able to have conversations even though she might not yet have any words, and she'll try to join in with simple songs. She'll be trying solids, and will enjoy putting food into her mouth with her fingers, turning her head to say 'no more' when she's had enough. She may try one or two familiar words, often

Timeline

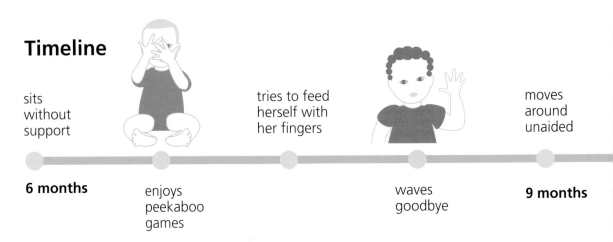

sits without support

tries to feed herself with her fingers

moves around unaided

6 months

enjoys peekaboo games

waves goodbye

9 months

'mama' or 'dada', and as she approaches 12 months she may begin to add one or two more; she's learning to connect words with objects.

By her first birthday your child has built sound foundations for propelling herself around the home, and she will be crawling, pulling herself up to stand and even taking those first few miraculous steps. She'll still enjoy learning about the world by putting objects in her mouth, but will also bang them together, drop them, grab, reach and point. Peekaboo is an important game at this age, and your child will love finding objects you've hidden underneath or behind things.

Emotionally, by the end of her first year, your child knows more about what she wants and is able to express her emotions to you. She'll feel more comfortable with you than with strangers.

This chapter includes plenty of activities to help your child explore movement and get to know the world as she approaches her first birthday – through massage, while being carried, in the bath and on the changing mat. It also offers ways for you to practise mindfulness yourself while your child is asleep or you're out walking with the buggy.

able to pick
up objects
with finger
and thumb

may
stand
without
support

uses one
or two words

12 months

Face-to-face focus

Eye-to-eye contact with another being is one of the most mindful of activities – and irresistible with a young baby who isn't yet talking. It's a key way to tune into one another and ask and answer questions even before language develops. In fact, this contact is the place where language acquisition starts.

1 Sitting propped up in bed or on a sofa, bend your knees and rest your baby's back and head against your thighs, so that your head and her head are at approximately the same height.

2 Say hello to your baby. Wait for her to respond. This might be with a sound or a gesture. At this age babies are just learning the mouth movements that go with different sounds.

3 Ask your baby a question. Again wait a little longer than you might usually do for a response.

4 Repeat the question or ask another one. Wait for a response then respond to it. Your baby is learning how to take turns. This is the essential skill underpinning the art of making conversation.

Baby massage

Try these soothing strokes after a bath or to help induce the relaxation essential before sleep. As you give your baby the massage, try not to think about what's coming up next in your day or to follow thoughts as they arise, guide your focus instead to the feel of your baby's skin, her eyes following you, and her perfect fingers and toes.

1 Place your baby on her back on a warmed towel. If she doesn't mind being naked, undress her. If this makes her unhappy, massage without oil, doing all the strokes in the sequence over her clothes. Kneel or sit in front of your baby's feet. Smile and talk to her, telling her what you're going to do.

2 If you are using oil, pour a little between your palms, rub them together, then place your fingers on your baby's hips. Stroke up her abdomen and chest, then out over her shoulders. Glide back down her arms to your starting position and repeat, building up a steady rhythm of strokes. You might like to sing or chant a nursery rhyme in time with your strokes.

You will need

- A warm room (26°C/80°F)
- A warm towel – one you're happy to spill oil on
- A little olive oil

3 Cupping the back of your baby's left arm with one hand, slide your other hand down from her under arm to her wrist. Repeat with your other hand. Repeat over and over, alternating hands each time. Again, aim to build up a rhythmic flow of strokes.

4 Take the back of your baby's left hand in your palm. Using your other thumb, stroke the palm, stretching out the fingers. Gently rotate each finger, squeezing lightly at the tip. Repeat steps 3 and 4 on your baby's right arm and hand.

5 Repeat steps 3 and 4 on her legs and feet.

6 Now turn your baby onto her front. If she finds this irritating, keep it brief. Repeat step 2, stroking up from her hips to her shoulders and gliding down the backs of her arms. If you are using oil, you may need to apply a little more to your hands at this point.

Tip box

■ Test the oil before using, do a patch test by dabbing a little on your baby's skin and checking for irritation after 24 hours. Warm the bottle by standing it in a mug of warm (not hot) water for a few minutes.

■ Don't start a massage if your baby seems hungry, fractious or overtired. And stop if she seems unhappy at any point.

SAFETY POINT ⚠ Once your baby is 6 months old she should enjoy more tummy time. But if she's younger always supervise her for short periods on her front, as in this massage sequence, and place her on her back for sleep.

7 Finish by placing your right palm on your baby's right shoulder. Stroke diagonally down her back and then down her left leg to her foot. As you lift your right hand away at the foot, stroke your left hand down from her left shoulder to her right foot. Build up a continuous flowing movement of diagonal strokes with both hands, and watch how your breathing gradually synchronises with your movements.

8 At the end of the massage, wrap your baby in the towel and give her a cuddle.

Other activity to try

Play a massage game with your baby's hands at any time of day. Rest the back of her hand in your palm and circle her palm with your thumb as you chant 'Round and round the garden like a teddy bear'. Then say 'One step, two step' while walking your fingertips up her arm, and 'Tickle you under there' as you gently tickle under her arm.

In the bath

If you think of bathtime as an opportunity to have fun with your baby, rather than a daily chore, you can lose yourself in play. The best fun of all comes when you climb into the bath, too, to chat, play water games and engage completely in your child's activities. Once your baby can sit unaided (usually between four and seven months), the fun really starts.

1 Climb into the bath yourself, checking the temperature (tepid body temperature is best) and have someone pass you your baby. Talk and smile as you lower her into the water with a cuddle. Tell her what you're going to do.

2 Sitting opposite each other, push a ball or float ducks towards each other. Name each object as you send it.

3 Fill a plastic pot with water and tip it over your knees. Then pour it over your baby's knees. Say the word 'knees'. Repeat, pouring the water over your shoulders, then your baby's shoulders, and finally over your heads, if she enjoys that.

You will need

- Balls and toy ducks
- Plastic pot (e.g. yogurt pot)
- Squeaky toys and squeezy toys
- Large warm towel

SAFETY POINT ⚠️ Never leave a baby or child alone in the bath, even for a few seconds. Gather everything you need before you start (towel, nappy, toys). If the phone or doorbell rings, ignore it, or take the infant with you to answer it.

4 Squeeze squeaky toys to make you both laugh. Or blast each other with squirty toys.

5 Try sub-aqua singing: put your lips in the water and hum or blow bubbles. Encourage your baby to copy you and sing together.

6 Bouncing games work well in the bath: sit your baby on your knee and 'drop' her into the water, or play Row the Boat, See-Saw or Horsey Horsey.

7 Before your child gets cold, bored or fractious, lift her out (it helps to have a partner handy) and wrap her in a warm fluffy towel for a cuddle.

Other activity to try

If your baby loves bathtime and splashy water games, look out for parent and baby swimming sessions. The confidence bath games instil is the first step towards making swimming a happy experience.

On the mat

Changing a baby can get rather monotonous! Use the plentiful opportunities on the mat to play with a mindful movement sequence. The giggles it elicits can bring back joy to the dullest moments of the day. This sequence is also great for freeing up babies who have been trapped in car seats and buggies for hours on end. It makes a good precursor to rough and tumble play when your child is older. It also allows you to enjoy valuable face-to-face time with your baby.

1 Place your baby on her back on a changing mat or a soft surface. Smile and talk to her; tell her what you're going to do. Take one of her hands in each of your hands. Open her arms out to the sides, keeping them in line with her shoulders.

2 Now cross your baby's arms over her chest. Repeat the arm opening and closing movement until your baby loosens up a bit. As she gets used to the action, stretch her arms very slightly at the open position, and press gently as you hold her arms crossed for a few seconds.

You will need

- Changing mat or comfortable surface such as a baby lambskin

Tip box ■ There's no need to undress your baby to follow this sequence; you can stretch her out and increase her mobility fully clothed.

SAFETY POINT ⚠ Don't force any movements if your baby resists them; keep everything gentle and fun.

(Change the cross of the arms each time you repeat the movement, alternating which arm is on top and which underneath).

3 Hold your baby's left hand in your left hand. Take her right ankle in your right hand. Slowly and carefully pull the limbs away from each other to create a slight diagonal stretch. Don't force the movement.

4 Bring your baby's left arm and right leg together so that her hand meets her opposite knee. Hold them together briefly, then pull them away from each other, holding the stretched position again briefly. Repeat the movement a few times.

5 Repeat the arm and leg stretch and touch sequence on the opposite limbs. This is good for brain development.

6 To finish the sequence, give your baby a big cuddle.

Mindful carrying

We tend to encase our babies in plastic to carry them around – clipped into car seats and strapped into buggies. As a result we all lose out on the physical stimulation and increased interaction that body-to-body connections bring. For babies, being carried may boost growth and development; for grown-ups, it makes you feel more confident as a parent.

1 Hold your baby with her back resting against your abdomen, looking outwards. Place one arm under and around her chest (with your thumb and index finger supporting her top shoulder) and her head resting on your forearm, if necessary. Take your other hand between her legs, so your palm comforts her abdomen.

2 Sway from side to side in this position or slowly walk around, swinging rhythmically from foot to foot so she can enjoy the motion.

Tip box ■ Babies who are carried regularly tend to cry less, spend more time quiet and alert and feed more often than those that aren't.

3 Hang your baby's arms over one forearm and lower her to your centre of gravity, with her back resting against your abdomen. Support beneath her buttocks, if necessary.

4 From this comfortable position, work on your own posture in a mindful way, to help relieve the stiff shoulders and stooping common in parents of young babies. Make sure your feet are hip-width apart, then align your knees over your ankles. Pull up your knees and thighs, hugging the muscle to the bones. Exhaling, lengthen your tailbone downwards and pull in your abdominal muscles to support your lower back.

5 Lift the sides of your waist, broaden your chest and align your shoulders over your hips. Draw your shoulder blades together and drop your shoulders away from your ears. Lift up from the back of your neck, as if you are being pulled up by a string from the crown of your head.

6 Try to hold the position for a few breaths, feeling your breath expanding in your abdomen and nurturing your baby with the connection.

Other activity to try

Use a sling or baby carrier for short trips out. As your baby gets older she might enjoy a frame backpack for an exciting view of the world.

6–12 months

Bedtime baby yoga pose

Babies are never too young for yoga – you don't need to be able to stand up to benefit from the poses. This sequence is calming for babies who suffer with digestive gripes and find it difficult to relax enough to go to sleep. As a parent, being able to do something active about colicky distress can boost confidence and positivity.

1 Place your baby on her back on a changing mat or the bed, and sit in front of her feet. Look her in the eyes, smile and talk to her; explain what you're going to do.

2 Take one of your baby's lower legs in each of your hands. Push your baby's knees in towards her stomach and apply gentle pressure. This is a wind-relieving pose! Hold briefly, then release. Repeat a few times.

3 Place the soles of her feet together, so her knees fall out to the sides. This is the reclining cobbler pose. Without moving her hips, circle her legs first clockwise and then anticlockwise.

You will need

• Changing mat or bed

Tip box ■ Talk to your baby as you massage or practise the yoga pose. This reassures her that you are really confident in handling her.

4 Stretch your baby's legs towards you, pulling them slightly and then dropping them gently to the mat or bed. Say 'relax' in a soothing voice as you do so. Repeat a few times.

5 Finally, place the palm of one hand horizontally over your baby's abdomen and rock your hand from side to side. Make the movement slow and smooth but keep the pressure firm (if you're too gentle it will feel tickly rather than comforting). Sing a lullaby as you do so.

Other activity to try

Try a gentle abdominal massage if your baby finds it comforting to be touched on her tummy. You can do this over her clothes, or with a little olive oil rubbed onto bare skin.

Gently circle the navel in a clockwise direction with your index and middle fingers. Let one hand make a full circle. The other makes a half-circle – lift it over the first hand when they meet. Gradually make wider circles to cover the abdominal region. Keep the rhythm steady and stroke confidently.

Walking meditation

Sometimes the only 'me time' you get as a parent is while walking a sleeping child in her buggy. Here, for just a moment, it's possible to find tranquillity in the midst of action, and it can be especially welcome if, like most parents of babies, you occasionally feel trapped. With each step savour the sense of purposeful autonomy walking brings and the freedom of the space above and around you.

1 As you begin to push the buggy, try to switch off from the minutiae of the day. This is your time now, so try not to think back over the day's events or anticipate what's coming next. Instead, just feel your breath flowing in and out of your body quite naturally.

2 Now guide your focus away from your inner world. Become aware of the world around you, especially the natural world: the sky and clouds, the temperature of the air, the signs of the season.

3 When thoughts arise, as they will, imagine them as clouds passing across a blue sky and allow them just to float on by. Find the blue sky between the clouds.

4 Become aware now of your pace: your feet lifting away from the ground and then finding it again, the length of your stride and how it co-ordinates with your breath. Feel the different parts of your feet against the ground: your heels, the balls of your feet, your toes as you push off. See how easily your weight shifts from side to side with each stride.

5 Finally, focus on your breathing. Inhale for four paces then exhale for four paces. Can you balance your inhalations and exhalations so they are the same length? Notice how your thoughts become steadied by the constancy of your pace.

Other activity to try

If you find it hard to still your mind while walking, try a counting exercise.

- -

Count to ten without allowing any thoughts to grab your attention. When you find yourself following a train of thought, go back to one and start the count again. Can you get past four? There will always be thoughts; you just have to ignore them and let them go on their way.

Hide and seek

The time-honoured game of hiding things and revealing them again – be it faces or other objects – will keep your child almost endlessly amused. It's also an important early bonding and learning activity, simultaneously introducing the concepts of things disappearing and reappearing. Your child will begin to understand that even though she can't see you, you will always be there for her.

1 Engage your child's attention, then hide your face behind your hands or a cloth.

2 Ask her where you've gone – this is important to engage her active curiosity.

3 Reveal yourself with a touch of drama – 'Peekaboo!' always works well.

4 Vary the time delay, facial expressions and accompanying noises to maintain the element of surprise, which encourages learning.

You will need

- Just your hands, or a small cloth

Other activity to try

You could hide behind furniture or try hiding a favourite toy and revealing it.

Tip box ■ Don't forget to let older children reverse the roles and have a go themselves. For younger children, you can hide and reveal their faces for them.

New you journal

6+ months

An approaching first birthday is a good time to think about the new you that has grown alongside your baby. You might consider who you are and how that has been influenced by your own childhood. Which qualities would you like to develop and which aren't so useful to you as a parent?

1 Start a journal, jotting down thoughts about your journey into parenthood whenever you have time. What has surprised you? What unexpected character traits have emerged? Can you recognise the voices and actions of your own parents in the way you parent? You don't have to write in full sentences; lists and notes are fine, or you may wish to doodle or draw your thoughts.

2 Now list the positives you've noticed in yourself over the past few months.

3 List the not-so-good characteristics that have emerged and which you'd like to let go of.

4 Finally, start a list of the character traits you'd like to make more of in the coming year. Don't feel you have to judge yourself on any of these lists. Change begins simply with awareness.

You will need

- Journal or pad of paper
- Pen or coloured pencils

Exploring senses

In the adult world the sense of sight dominates the other senses, but mindfulness encourages us to bring attention to all the senses equally. Playing with babies and toddlers helps us to do just that because it highlights the key role all the senses have in the development of a young child. For young children, the senses are natural tools of learning. Think how a baby wants to explore new objects orally or how a toddler's fingers constantly move over surfaces. This is their way of investigating and discovering the world around them – and when you play beside them, you gain a new appreciation of that world, too. In the following chapter you will find a variety of activities to help you explore all the senses together.

Mindful timeline: 1–1½ years

Between the ages of 12 and 18 months, your child can do more and more for himself. By his first birthday, he should be able to stand on his own and begin to walk without support. He can soon transfer small objects to another person using his thumb and one finger. His attempts at communication and making conversation have begun in earnest. Emotionally, your child starts to develop empathy, vital to building relationships. Alongside this, separation anxiety grows: he feels so strongly attached to you that he can be upset when you're not there. Playing mindfully with your child offers reassurance.

Your child's understanding will have increased to the extent that he now knows who that person is staring back at him in the mirror. He is developing much stronger preferences for people and toys now, and he is imitating people during play. At this stage your child favours the person who looks after him most above all others.

Having completed his graduation from liquid to solid food, he will start to be able

Timeline

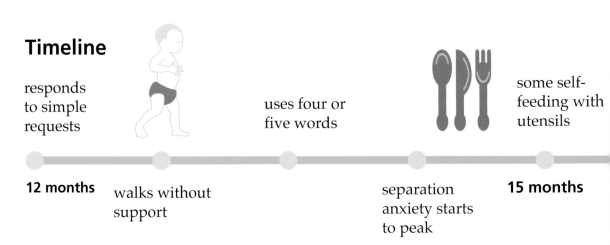

responds to simple requests

uses four or five words

some self-feeding with utensils

12 months

walks without support

separation anxiety starts to peak

15 months

to feed himself with a spoon, and should be well able to drink from a cup. When he speaks he is comfortable using four or five words; as he approaches 18 months old this may be increasing to sentences of five to ten words.

By 18 months your child's developments in strength, stability and co-ordination mean that he can now pull toys with wheels, as well as being able to place objects into containers and then take them out again. The very beginnings of artistic endeavour are witnessed for the first time now he can use crayons to make a mark on paper. His spoken vocabulary will have increased to as many as ten words and he can understand easy direction given to him, such as 'eat your food'.

This chapter seeks to explore your child's early sensory awareness. At this young age, he will be excited to engage with different textures, shapes and sounds, even though he doesn't yet have the vocabulary to express them. The activities in this chapter will encourage him to explore different textures in the Sensory trail and match objects with sounds in the Guess the sound game, while a Bedtime massage allows both of you to enjoy mindful movement as a wind-down before sleep.

uses five to ten words

marks paper with crayons

pulls toys on wheels

18 months

Sensory trail

Everyone enjoys the sensation of walking on grass with bare feet, and for young children this pleasure is doubled because they have a heightened sense of touch. In this next activity you lay out a sensory trail of different textures for your child to explore and develop their sense of touch. It also has the advantage of developing balancing skills in newly toddling babies.

You will need

- Large indoor or outdoor space
- Variety of surfaces with different textures, e.g.:
  - 4 cushions of any size (if possible, choose cushions with different fabrics)
  - Carpet samples (from your local carpet shop)
  - Small rug
  - Doormat (make sure it's not rough)

1 Lay a straight path with your chosen items, each of which should have a different texture.

2 Demonstrate to your child how you would like him to crawl or walk along the path, with arms outstretched to help him balance.

3 Let your child have a go.

4 He will need your support at first, so begin by holding each hand if he is walking. When he is more confident, let him try a few steps by himself, but stay close by in case you need to steady him again.

5 Walking over the cushions will be the trickiest part, so a steadying hand from you will be required for this, or encourage him to crawl over the cushions.

Other activities to try

After your child has mastered the path, change the order of the surfaces and introduce some new ones.

Progress from a straight path to a wavy one.

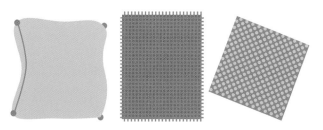

Tip box   ▪ Let your child repeat the path trail as many times as he wishes.

Touch and texture game

Of all the senses, touch is the most predominant in the under-twos. With hands outstretched, they explore the world's textures with their fingertips. With time, they begin to associate different textures with people, places and times of day. A soft fluffy blanket means security and bedtime, while a smooth shiny raincoat says it's raining. This very adaptable game can be graduated to suit all ages, and while you're playing, reflect on 'seeing' the world afresh through touch.

You will need

- Container or basket big enough to hold all the objects
- 6–8 hard and soft objects (for example, wood, plastic or fabric)

1 With the basket in front of you and your child to your left, take a hard object out of the basket. Put it on the left. Then take out a soft object, and put it on the right.

2 Press your fingertips into the hard object and say the word 'hard'. Repeat the action with the soft object, saying the word 'soft'.

3 Pass both objects to your child, and invite him to feel the surfaces, as you did.

4 As he holds each object, say the words 'hard' and 'soft' again. Younger children will not be able to name these textures at first, but as your child continues to play the game, the words will become more familiar.

5 Invite older children to sort the rest of the objects in the container into the hard or soft pile.

Other activities to try

Try using objects with different textural opposites, like rough and smooth.

Choose objects with contrasting temperatures, like cork, wool, marble, wood and stone. Show your child how to sort objects by temperature: warm and cold.

Graduate from two groups to three groups for sorting.

As your child gains in confidence, he might like to try the game with his eyes closed or wearing a blindfold, but remember you will need to show him first.

Gardens and parks are a great source of objects: crisp autumn leaves, knobbly pine cones and gnarled pieces of bark to name a few.

Tip box   ■ Choose contrasting objects so your child can clearly feel the difference between hard and soft.

■ Don't be alarmed if your child doesn't pick up on the words straight away. It can take time to absorb new language.

Guess the sound game

Try this experiment in mindfulness: stop and count how many sounds you can hear. First listen to the sounds close to you, then tune in to those far away. Notice how many sounds we usually blank out because the brain finds them familiar. For a child, most of these sounds are unknowns waiting to be identified. Hearing is a sensory tool that helps children build understanding of the world around them.

This fun game highlights the sense of hearing and helps children build their knowledge of different sounds. The extra activities encourage them to identify sounds, refining their ability to listen.

1 Ask your child to sit on your left and place the tray in front of you. Put the objects on the tray.

2 Say to your child, 'We are going to play a guess the sound game'. Point to and name out loud all the different objects on the tray.

You will need

- Tray
- 3 objects your child is familiar with that make distinctly different sounds (for example, metal or wooden spoons knocked together, a shaken packet of cereal)
- Cloth, such as a tea towel, big enough to cover the tray

Tip box

■ It's a good idea not to use musical instruments in this project as they could distract from the game.

■ Tell your child to take time to really listen to the sound before making their guess.

3 Cover the tray with the cloth. Select something under the cloth, for example, two spoons. Knock them together, asking your child to listen to the sound.

Other activities to try

As your child becomes more confident, add extra objects, to a maximum of 6, and start to introduce new objects with unfamiliar sounds.

As he grows older and more familiar with the objects and their names, ask him to try to guess which object he thinks made the noise.

Once older children have mastered the game, keep the cloth over the tray. If your child gets stuck, verbally name the object to give him a clue.

4 Remove the cloth and name the object out loud, then pick it up to show your child.

5 Invite your child to make the same sound so he can clearly see which object makes that sound. Repeat with all the objects on the tray.

Toddler yoga

If you've tried doing yoga with children in the room you'll know how they delight in trying to copy you, so this easy routine is for you to enjoy together. Yoga is great for children, encouraging co-ordination, concentration and self-awareness. For parents, it makes you focus on the moment at hand. Do this sequence with your child, encouraging him to copy you.

1 Kneel with your buttocks on your heels. Walk your hands forwards until your chest rests on your thighs, arms extended in front of you. Tell your child you are seeds growing into a tree.

2 Now press into your hands, rock back on your heels and, breathing out, gradually roll up until you are standing, bringing your head up last. Inhaling, extend your arms above your head. Bend to the left, then the right like the branches of a tree.

3 Flop forward from the hips like a scarecrow, neck and head relaxed and arms hanging loosely. You may need to bend your knees.

Tip box ▥ Encourage your child to do yoga with a doll or teddy.

4 Place your hands on the floor and step or jump both feet backwards so you make an inverted V-shape, bottom high in the air and arms and legs stretching out. Push back on your hands, take your buttocks up and towards the back of the room and relax your heels towards the floor like a dog stretching. Make howling dog noises.

5 Come down to all fours, making a table shape. Then bend your elbows and lower your chest to the floor and stretch your legs back. Place your palms beneath your shoulders and press your chest forwards and up. You are a snake now, so make snakey sounds.

6 Push back on your hands to return your buttocks to your heels. Have your child place his hands on your lower back to feel your breath moving in and out. Do the same for him.

7 To finish, press your palms together in front of your heart and bow to each other.

Other activity to try

Kids love face yoga – try the Lion Pose: open your mouth wide, stick your tongue out, make your eyes as big as you can and breathe audibly.

Bedtime massage

Young children love having their legs and feet rubbed, so this routine makes a comforting way to begin a bedtime wind down. As you relax into the flow, co-ordinate your breathing with the movement of strokes – this is mindfulness in motion.

1 Have your child lie comfortably on his back facing you, with his legs and feet uncovered. Warm a little olive oil between your palms.

2 Wrap your left hand around the back of your child's left thigh and gently pull down the upper and lower leg (releasing pressure at the knee). When you reach the ankle, repeat the stroke with your other hand, building up a slow and steady flow of strokes and alternating hands.

3 Take your child's left foot in one hand and his calf in the other. Rotate the ankle in one direction, and then in the opposite direction.

You will need

- Warm room (26°C/80°F)
- A little olive oil: before using, do a patch test by dabbing a small amount on your child's skin and checking for irritation after 24 hours.

Tip box ▪ Stop if your child cries or seems distracted or too tired to enjoy the massage.

4 Sandwich the foot between your hands. Stroke your top hand down the upper part of the foot and away at the toes. Repeat, building up a flowing movement.

5 Cup the top of the foot with your fingers and rub one thumb, then the other up the sole and out beneath the toes in a T-shape. Keep the strokes rhythmic.

6 Squeeze each toe from base to tip, then rotate the toes, pulling away at the tip. Repeat all the steps on your child's right leg and foot.

Mirror fun

Mirrors are an endlessly useful tool in mindful play – they double the fun and the learning possibilities. This mirror activity and its many variations help to build vocabulary and communication skills, as well as concepts of self-awareness, which are all invaluable for your child's development.

1 Settle on the floor with your child in your lap, making sure you are both clearly reflected in the mirror. You can also lay the mirror flat on the floor and look into it from above.

2 Start a question and answer routine, using the mirror. 'What's this?' 'It's your nose.' 'Where's your nose?' 'There's your nose!'

3 Continue with the routine, covering all parts of the face. You can then move on to expressions, such as sad, happy, angry, tired or silly.

4 Let the game develop as long as your child stays interested by your actions.

You will need

- Good-sized mirror
- Scarf (optional)
- Favourite toys (optional)

Other activities to try

Try hanging up a small mirror on some string so that it can spin around – your child will be able to see the reflections from different angles, as well as the different light reflections.

Use a scarf to play peekaboo – your child will be even more engaged when it's himself he's looking at.

You can do any number of actions and get your child to copy you; such as pointing, grabbing or lifting.

Patience meditation

1+ years

Patience is a skill most parents practise most days. Welcome practice sessions as a way of gaining perspective and learning not to react to triggers. Pausing to breathe gives you space to recognise different points of view and new ways of tackling problems.

1 Whenever you need to take time out from thinking try this exercise that helps you pause before reacting. Sit comfortably and close your eyes.

2 Breathe in for a count of two, hold the breath for a moment, then breathe in for another count of two. Hold again, then breathe in for a final count of two. Let the breath out in one long, slow flow, visualising unhelpful thoughts and feelings exiting with the breath.

3 Repeat, breathing into your belly for a count of two, pause, then breathe into the sides of your chest for a count of two, pause, then breathe in up to your collar-bones for a count of two. Exhale in a smooth and continuous flow.

4 Keep breathing in this way, filling yourself with a positive flow of energising oxygen and sensing how much space there is in your body.

Co-ordination

We take very much for granted the ability to move our bodies. The degree of complexity of co-ordination involved in playing sports and the finer motor skills of using a keyboard or threading a needle in some ways defines who we are. Having specialised in teaching PE, I have observed children derive as much pleasure from mastering new physical skills as any language achievement. Control of their bodies gives them a sense of empowerment and self-confidence. In the following chapter you will find physical activities that allow you and your child to experience mindfulness by co-ordinating body and brain.

Mindful timeline: 1½–2 years

In the six months leading up to her second birthday you will see your child's walking begin to improve, and by two, she may even be able to run. Her increased mobility means she may now manage to climb up, and later down, a stair with the support of a hand or rail. She will also be able to respond to more complex requests and follow two-step commands. Emotionally, your child is connecting feelings with words and experiencing new emotions such as frustration, which can be confusing and result in tantrums. Mindful activities can be a calming distraction.

Your child's speech will have developed so that she will begin to regularly use two or three words together to make sentences and requests of her own, such as 'more juice please'.

She will also now have developed a sense of the familiar and will notice if things are out of their regular place, so if for example the picture on her bedroom wall is the wrong way around she will notice.

Timeline

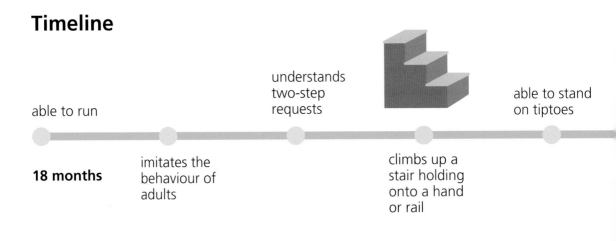

understands two-step requests

able to run

able to stand on tiptoes

18 months

imitates the behaviour of adults

climbs up a stair holding onto a hand or rail

Her sense of balance will be continually improving; she will begin to be able to stand on her tiptoes and by her second birthday should be able to kick a large ball. Her increasing manual dexterity means she can now turn thin paper pages in a book.

With the honing of her observational skills comes the imitation of the behaviour of others, in particular adults and older children who are obviously important influences in your child's life.

The activities on the following pages focus on the early stages and development of your child's co-ordination, encouraging manual dexterity, balance and general co-ordination. A game such as Where does it go? will not only improve your child's hand-eye co-ordination and encourage her recognition of different shapes, it is also a great introduction to doing simple puzzles. Puzzles have always been a means towards mindfulness in the Buddhist tradition, used as a way of focusing the mind on the matter in hand and introducing new ways of seeing the world.

21 months

turns thin
paper pages
in a book

kicks a
large ball

uses two or
three words
together

24 months

Where does it go?

Hand-eye co-ordination can be built up from the earliest stages with games that involve the simplest puzzling tasks, starting with fitting squares together and moving towards the more traditional endeavour of making a picture from the separate pieces. This activity shows you how to create materials for the most basic 3D puzzle, which can be developed as your child's skills improve.

You will need

- Collection of different-shaped objects or building blocks, such as a triangle, a square and a circle
- Cardboard box
- Scissors or craft knife

1 Gather together a number of different-shaped building blocks, such as a triangle, a square and a circle.

2 Cut holes in the top of the cardboard box that are the same shape as the blocks you have chosen, but make the holes slightly larger. Tape up any open flaps so that there is no other way in except through the holes.

3 Give the first shape to your child. Guide her fingers around the edges, so that she traces the outline of the shape, and then do the same around the hole in the box so that she becomes familiar with the feel of the shape.

4 Ask her to put the shape through the matching hole. If she has trouble finding the correct one, guide her to it.

5 Repeat steps 3 and 4 with the rest of the shapes you have made. When your child is more confident, start again, and see if she can find the correct holes for the shapes on her own.

6 Once your child is more familiar with the shapes you are using, start to introduce language. When you pass her the shape, say what it is, and relate it back to her knowledge of the way it feels. For example, 'This is a triangle. The triangle has three sides.'

Other activity to try

Once this has been mastered, you can create variations in the size and shape of the holes and corresponding objects, ideally on the same box, so that the task presents your child with more of a challenge.

Bean bag throwing

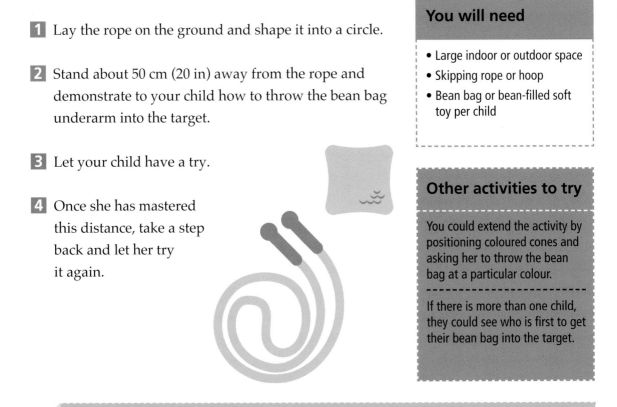

1½–2 years

Bean bags are one of the best pieces of equipment to help young children develop their throwing skills. Unlike a ball, bean bags won't roll away from them, so they feel nice and secure. In this activity the target area for throwing the bean bag is defined to help hand-eye co-ordination and focus attention.

1 Lay the rope on the ground and shape it into a circle.

2 Stand about 50 cm (20 in) away from the rope and demonstrate to your child how to throw the bean bag underarm into the target.

3 Let your child have a try.

4 Once she has mastered this distance, take a step back and let her try it again.

You will need

- Large indoor or outdoor space
- Skipping rope or hoop
- Bean bag or bean-filled soft toy per child

Other activities to try

You could extend the activity by positioning coloured cones and asking her to throw the bean bag at a particular colour.

If there is more than one child, they could see who is first to get their bean bag into the target.

Tip box ■ Remind your child that she needs to keep her arm straight when throwing.

Roll a ball

1½–2 years

This lovely face-to-face game helps to develop focused attention and co-operation as you send and receive a ball between yourselves using a rolling action. It's also a great activity for starting to build the gross motor skills and hand-eye co-ordination required for catching a ball.

1 Sit on the floor with your legs apart so that you are face to face with your child.

2 Invite your child to sit in the same way. By sitting like this you are defining an area and making a barrier for the ball.

3 Begin by gently rolling the ball to your child.

4 Encourage her to stop the ball with her hands. If it is necessary, demonstrate what to do.

5 Invite her to roll the ball back to you.

6 When your child becomes confident in passing the ball, move yourself back a little. Repeat this step when she gains confidence at this new distance.

You will need

- Beach ball or similarly large and light ball

Other activity to try

Once your child has mastered this activity with a beach ball, try it with a smaller ball.

Tip box ■ Before you roll the ball to your child, briefly look down and then look at her so she makes the association with looking to the sending point.

Cardboard tube threading

Mindfulness is about becoming absorbed in an activity, and your child will find this simple activity endlessly absorbing. It also provides another opportunity for developing hand-eye co-ordination and strengthening the finger muscles. There's the added advantage that it's a very easy game to prepare.

You will need

- Cardboard tube (the type inside a roll of kitchen paper)
- Small bell or any small object wider than the end of the cardboard tube
- Cord or chain about 1 m (3 ft) in length (you could use the cord from a dressing gown)
- Knife to cut the tube

1 Start by tying the bell or small object to one end of the cord or chain. This acts as a stop for the tube and also prevents it from coming off the cord or chain.

2 Place the cord or chain with the attached bell or small object on the floor or on a low table.

3 Cut the tube in half. Describe to your child what you are doing and why.

4 Demonstrate to your child how to thread the short tube onto the cord or chain and slide it back and forth.

5 Remove the tube from the cord or chain and allow your child to have a try.

Other activity to try

Once your child has mastered threading a tube, she is ready to move on to threading pasta onto a cord. Use rigatoni (tube-shaped) pasta and a piece of string about 50 cm (20 in) in length. Tie a piece of pasta to the end of the string and knot it to form a stop before your child starts threading.

Tip box   ■ When you are demonstrating this activity make sure your child is sitting to your left so she has an unrestricted view of your hands. If your child is left-handed, you will need to demonstrate with your left hand, with your child sitting on your right side.

Circus performer

We have five senses but in some ways balance is like a child's sixth sense. Young children seem to have within them an innate longing to develop their balance and they take any opportunity given to them to walk low beams or along low walls. This activity allows them to pretend to be a circus performer, walking a tightrope, but in complete safety.

1. Find a stone-paved or concrete area where you are able to chalk onto the surface (and rub the chalk away after finishing the activity).

2. Draw a straight line on the ground with the chalk, about 3 m (10 ft) in length.

You will need

- Large outdoor space
- Piece of coloured chalk

3 Demonstrate to your child how to walk along the chalk line, putting one foot directly in front of the other. Walk in an upright position, eyes looking forwards, chest open and arms stretched out horizontally.

4 Encourage your child to have a turn at walking along the line, or 'tightrope'. She will need your support to guide him in a straight line, so keep hold of both of her outstretched hands as she walks along.

Other activities to try

When your child is confident walking the line, she could try holding two flags in each hand. She could also try carrying a small bell, which she has to try not to let ring while walking.

When your child is ready to progress to walking along a low beam or brick wall, let her choose the beam she wants to start with. Children have a very good sense of what height they feel comfortable with.

Building a tower

Constructing a tower of building blocks in a prescribed order is a real challenge for your child, and when she achieves it a major accomplishment. In this activity, you build a tower first, and if you use slow mindful movements, your child will follow your example. This encourages hand-eye co-ordination while strengthening muscular finger development and introducing the concept of ordering by shape and size.

1 Ask your child to help you take the building blocks to a clear area on the floor.

2 Sit down with your child on your left, and the blocks slightly to your right.

3 Tell your child that you are going to build the blocks into a tower. Select the largest block and put it in front of you in the centre, then complete the rest of the tower with slow, considered movements, working up to the smallest block at the top.

You will need

- 5–10 building blocks graduated in size (ideally some should be big enough to require your child to carry them with both hands)

Tip box

■ Start with 3 or 5 blocks and build up gradually to 10.

■ Just building a tower is an accomplishment for the youngest children, so don't panic if your child cannot achieve a graduated effect. In time she will come to recognise that the blocks need to be graduated in size.

Other activities to try

Build the tower again, but this time stack the blocks up one corner rather than centrally.

- -

Use the blocks to build a horizontal stair going left to right, smallest to largest.

- -

You could also try this activity using stacking rings with a rod up the middle.

4 Tell your child that you are going to dismantle the tower so she can build it.

5 Take down the blocks carefully, one at a time, and place them to the right of your child (she can help you do this). Invite her to build the tower herself.

Push and bend

1½+ years

This activity uses the same skills of co-ordination and concentration as Building a tower but with added colour and the tactile bendiness of pipe cleaners. Don't worry if your child just wants to swing the pipe cleaners around her head, bend them or wrap them around things. They're so engrossing to play with you might find yourself doing that, too!

1 Place the colander on the floor upside down, so the bottom is uppermost.

2 Pick up a pipe cleaner and say its colour. Explain to your child that you are going to push the pipe cleaner into a hole.

3 Show your child how to position the end of the pipe cleaner in the hole and push it through.

4 Ask her to pick a pipe cleaner to poke into the colander. You might like to repeat the colours of the pipe cleaners as she chooses.

5 Let her repeat until she has made a hedgehog of pipe cleaners. Then have fun bending the wires to make creative shapes.

You will need

- A packet of coloured pipe cleaners
- A metal or plastic colander with large holes

Stillness meditation

The months running up to a child's second birthday are very busy. This action and inaction exercise forces you to stop doing and appreciate some stillness. Your child will love performing it with you, but it will feel more peaceful if you practise by yourself.

1 When in the middle of a hectic round of activity and at your most physically busy, stop for a moment, quickly spin around on the spot 3 to 5 times, then lie on your back on the floor.

2 Simply lie there, spreading your arms and legs wide. Make space between your toes. Turn your palms to the sky and stretch your fingers wide. Broaden your gaze, as if looking out through your temples, allowing your eyesight to soften.

3 Hold the position for up to 5 minutes, feeling the world settle around you and appreciating the ground firmly supporting your weight. This stillness is always there amid the madness of the turning world.

4 When you are ready to get up and go again, roll onto one side and rest for a moment before pushing up to a sitting position.

Arts and crafts

Love of creating seems to be an innate desire that is within all of us from the very earliest of ages. If young children are encouraged in their creative endeavours, it provides an important source of self-confidence and satisfaction. It matters not that you may only see blobs of colour on a page because for children it is their way of making their mark and saying who they are. In the following chapter you will find a variety of art and craft activities that will satisfy every young budding artist and occupy both of you in mindful creativity.

Mindful timeline: 2–2½ years

Unlike at his first birthday, your child will be actively aware of his second birthday. Over the next six months he will continue to develop his early basic skills, for example, beginning to sort objects into categories of shape and colour. Your child may start potty training at any time between 18 months and 3 years. These are key months for emotional development. Your toddler experiences big emotions he may not be able to express, from anger to guilt, and practising mindfulness will help you cope with the everyday petty frustrations and upsets this brings.

From the age of two upwards your child may also be learning how to ride a small tricycle, although this skill can be very variable as some children will find the alternating motion more difficult to master.

At this age your child will begin to enjoy being around and playing with other children, although co-operative play and taking turns will come later, so there may still be fights over particular favoured

Timeline

begins to sort objects by shape and colour

potty training

24 months

enjoys playing with other children

beginnings of make-believe play

toys. At this point you may also notice the beginnings of make-believe play as your child begins to use his imagination.

Routine is very important to children at this age. While he will not really understand the concept of times and routines, your child is likely to notice and protest at any big changes to his daily schedule. So, for example, if you go on holiday it is vital that bedtime and mealtimes remain as normal as possible, otherwise excitement at being in a new place may well boil over into tantrums.

Art and craft activities can be extremely important in encouraging your child's development, not just for increasing his knowledge of colours and his manual skills holding crayons and scissors, but for exercising his imagination and creative output. Try not to worry about the inevitable mess; being patient while your child is creating – particularly getting painty hands with Hands on art – is all part of being a mindful parent at this stage in his development. Listen and talk to your child as he makes Angel fish handprints or enjoys constructing Floating fun toys to play with at bath time. And don't forget to praise the art he creates. This shows him just how much you value his imagination.

starts to ride a tricycle

able to throw a ball overhand

27 months

objects to big changes in routine

30 months

Painting with water

When children paint they are usually confined to a sheet of paper, but if you move the activity outdoors and use water, every surface can be their canvas. For parents, this activity is about letting go. Don't worry about the lack of paint; children are happy simply to make their mark. No need to stress about mess either since there's no clearing up!

1 Pour some water into the container. Once you are outdoors, explain to your child that he is going to paint, but instead of using paint on paper, he can paint with water on any surface he likes, such as a tree trunk.

2 Hand your child a paintbrush and water and watch him create.

You will need

- Paintbrush (such as a small brush for painting woodwork) per child
- Container for the water, preferably with a handle

Tip box ■ If there are no-go areas in your outdoor space, give very clear instructions about where your child is allowed to roam.

Floor art

This brilliant activity gives children space to get creative; they are not restricted to a regular size or shape of paper. And who says only hands can draw? Feet dipped in paint might be just as good, and will encourage different approaches to creativity.

1 Clear as much floor space as you can and cover it with the paper. The point of this project is to have an adventure exploring and marking the paper, without the usual limits.

2 Tape the paper to a clean area of floor (preferably linoleum or other wipe-clean surface). Make sure the area is free from hazards and valuable furniture.

3 Line up the art materials and let your child choose one. Direct him to the paper; he may be a little hesitant at first.

4 Don't be afraid to join in; lose yourselves in creating patterns and stories together.

You will need

- Poster paper
- Masking tape
- Crayons, felt-tip pens, paint

Hands on

Children love the sensation of covering their hands with paint, and this activity lets them do exactly that. They make handprints using paint and then turn them into a piece of art.

You will need

- Plastic tablecloth or newspaper
- Poster or powder paint mixed thickly in 2 or 3 bright colours of your choice
- Pots to mix up powder paint
- Apron for each child
- 2 sheets of A3-sized paper per paint colour
- Plastic tray or shallow dish for each colour
- Spoons for mixing
- Area to spread the paper when drying
- Scissors

1 Cover your work surface with the cloth or newspaper.

2 If using powder paint, mix with water to make a paint that has the consistency of household paint.

3 Explain to your child that he is going to be doing some handprints.

4 Ask him to put on his apron.

5 Put the A3 paper and the trays on the table.

6 Start with one colour and let him help to pour it into a tray. Spread it out using the back of a spoon.

7 Ask him to spread out his hand and put it into the paint, and then transfer it to the paper.

8 Repeat the process until you have two sheets of paper covered with handprints.

9 Ask your child to wash his hands and start all over again with a new colour.

10 When all the sheets of paper are covered with handprints, allow them to dry.

Tip box	■ Don't use blue paint for the handprints if you will be using your child's handprints for the Angel fish handprint activity on page 88 because the background for that will be blue.

Angel fish handprints

Taking a collection of your child's handprints, you can turn them into a new piece of art – like these angel fish made from cut-outs of the handprints made in the activity on page 86.

1 Place the wallpaper-lining paper on a table and weigh it down at the corners.

2 Mix up the blue powder paint or water down the poster paint to a wash consistency.

3 Using the sponge, show your child how to dip it in the paint and then spread it onto the paper with a sweeping wave action.

4 When all the paper is covered with the blue wash, allow it to dry.

5 Take one of the cut-out handprints and ask your child to put glue on the un-painted side of the palm.

You will need

- Wallpaper-lining paper or butcher's paper, about 80–100 cm (31–40 in)
- Blue poster or powder paint
- Household sponge cut into about 10 cm (4 in) square
- Area to spread the paper when drying
- Cut-out handprints (see pages 86–87)
- Glue stick
- Coloured felt-tip pens

Tip box ■ Remember to let your child go at his own pace. It might take several stages to complete the activity.

6 Let him stick it anywhere on the blue painted paper.

7 Take another hand in another colour and stick it on top of the first hand with a slight overlap, ensuring that you have the fingers all going in the same way.

8 If you have a third colour, repeat with that.

9 The overlapping fingers on the handprint should give the impression of a feathery fan.

10 Let your child make several fish to fill the blue area.

11 Show him how he can make eyes on the fish using the felt-tip pens.

12 When it is finished, pin up the artwork so he can admire his handiwork.

Other activities to try

Of course, the possibilities are endless for decorating the fish. You might like to use shells, seaweed and/or glitter paint.

You might like to read together the story *The Rainbow Fish* by Marcus Pfister before or after doing this activity.

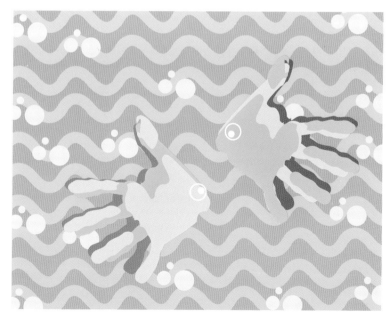

Potato prints

2–2½ years

Gloriously messy and fun, this activity provides an opportunity for your child to explore colours and textures while creating beautiful printed patterns.

1 Wash the potatoes and dry them.

2 Prepare your area for painting by laying down newspaper and squeezing the paint into shallow trays. Wear old clothes or an apron.

3 Cut the potatoes in half and show your child how to dip them in the paint and press them gently onto the paper.

4 Let him experiment with the colours and with the different patterns provided by the potatoes.

5 Invite your child to pin the prints to the wall once they are dry.

You will need

- Baking potatoes
- Newspaper
- Water-based paint in different colours
- Shallow trays
- Knife
- Large sheets of paper

Tip box ■ Once your child has done this activity with the natural shape of the potato, try carving into it with a knife to create more interesting shapes.

Homemade play dough

There is no better way to strengthen finger muscles than by playing with dough – and you get to make your own here, providing parents with a mindful focus all your own.

You will need

- 120 g plain flour
- 150 g salt
- 2 teaspoons cream of tartar
- 240 ml water
- 1 teaspoon food colouring
- 2 teaspoons cooking oil
- Medium saucepan
- Wooden spoon
- Rolling pin
- Plastic knife

1 Put the flour, salt and cream of tartar into a medium saucepan and stir together with a wooden spoon.

2 Over a medium heat, gradually stir in the water, food colouring and oil. Stir continually as the mixture begins to cook and forms into a sticky ball.

3 Remove from the heat and allow to cool for 15–30 minutes.

4 Ask your child to put on an apron, lay a cloth and help you set out the tools.

5 Have fun rolling, coiling, pressing and cutting dough.

Tip box
- The dough can be stored for several days in a plastic bag in the fridge.
- Explain to your child that dough is not to be eaten.

Finger fun

We take our hands and the skills we employ them for very much for granted; for a child, hands are a key tool in their development. This next activity is a fun art project which, when completed, can be used in both language and counting activities. It requires little more than a pair of old gloves and some Velcro.

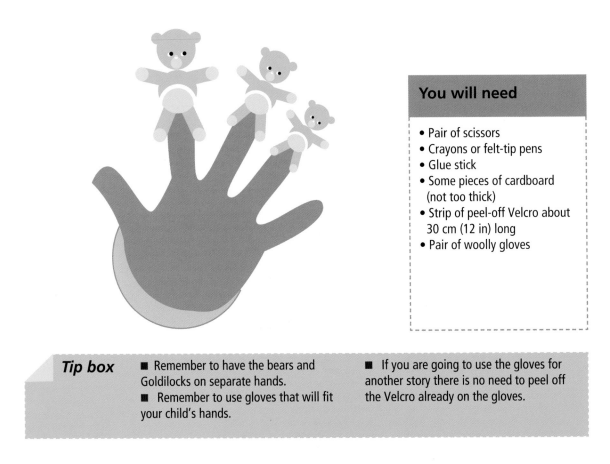

You will need

- Pair of scissors
- Crayons or felt-tip pens
- Glue stick
- Some pieces of cardboard (not too thick)
- Strip of peel-off Velcro about 30 cm (12 in) long
- Pair of woolly gloves

Tip box
- Remember to have the bears and Goldilocks on separate hands.
- Remember to use gloves that will fit your child's hands.

- If you are going to use the gloves for another story there is no need to peel off the Velcro already on the gloves.

Story gloves

1 At the back of the book on page 156 you will find
the characters for the story Goldilocks and the Three
Bears. Photocopy this page and cut out the figures.

2 Ask your child to colour in the figures.

3 Ask him to stick the figures onto the cardboard and
allow the glue to dry.

4 Cut out the figures.

5 Cut the Velcro into 2-cm (1 in) pieces.

6 Stick the Velcro on one side at the back of the figure,
and the other corresponding piece on a finger of one
of the gloves.

7 Repeat until all the figures have been backed with
Velcro, with corresponding pieces on the gloves.

8 The gloves are now ready to be used for a
storytelling session of Goldilocks and the
Three Bears.

Other activity to try

The Story gloves can be used
for many other stories, here
are just a few suggestions:
The Three Billy Goats Gruff;
The Three Little Pigs; Little Red
Riding Hood.

Floating fun

Children like having toys to play with in the bath, and this activity adds to the fun, letting them create their own toys while at the same time learning about objects that sink and float.

1 Gather your materials on the floor or a low table. Invite your child to sit with you.

2 Ask him 'What floats in water?' He might reply 'boats', or with the names of marine animals.

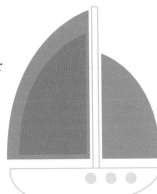

3 Draw his ideas onto the polystyrene and cut them out with the craft knife, being careful to keep your child's hands out of the way.

4 Use the skewer to make a hole in each object and let your child thread them together to form a flotilla.

5 At bathtime, set the flotilla off and let your child play with the creation, trying to sink it with waves and marvelling as it floats to the surface.

SAFETY POINT ! Never leave your child unaccompanied around water, even for a short period.

You will need

- Pieces of polystyrene
- Pen
- Craft knife
- Skewer
- String
- Full bathtub

Other activity to try

Emphasise the contrast between floating and sinking objects by bringing some heavy ones along to bathtime. Drop them in the water and explore their journey with your child.

This activity doesn't have to be restricted to bathtime. If you have a pond in your garden or nearby, take your flotilla on an adventure there too.

Tidy-up time meditation

Playtime with a toddler is not about minimalist perfectionism. But some mindful decluttering at the end of a play session makes a space seem more serene and encourages children to care for possessions.

1 Make a special place for every toy and give it its own distinctive container: farm animals in a basket, balls in a box, stacking toys on a shelf and so on.

2 Make a game of tidying up at the end of a play session, allowing enough time for it. Explain to your child what you're going to do.

3 Encourage your child to identify a single type of toy, work out where it lives and take it there. Or offer a little container so he can gather a few toys at a time.

4 Offer a mini dustpan so he can brush up afterwards. Tidying lets a child feel pride in his special things.

You will need

- Lots of small storage containers, one for each type of toy
- Small dustpan and brush

Mindful games and movement

Is there any greater joy for a child than the joy of moving to music or the thrill of a game in which they get to use their imagination? These quite simple mindful pleasures can go a long way towards helping your child's development, too – they encourage not only co-ordination and listening skills, but the ability to follow and remember instructions and, importantly, to co-operate with others. In the following chapter you will find everything from dancing with balloons to making your own skittle alley.

Mindful timeline: 2½–3 years

In the months leading up to her third birthday, your child is becoming increasingly mobile, and may now be able to walk up and down stairs holding the banister. Her dexterity will have improved to the extent that she can use children's scissors and may be able to help dress herself. Emotionally, your child will probably be developing an awareness of how her feelings and behaviour and yours as parents affect each other. Mindfulness helps you develop the patience and understanding that builds a calm, positive environment as she explores the world.

By now your child's sense of adventure will have been boosted by the ability to open doors, so she could be anywhere! This means that you will need to keep a close eye on her, and keep any doors you don't want her to go through firmly locked, so that her adventures don't lead her outside the house without your knowledge. The honing of her motor skills means that she will now be able to stack objects in size order. Potty training should now be in full swing and she will certainly be advanced

Timeline

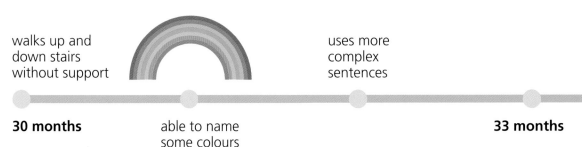

walks up and down stairs without support

30 months

able to name some colours

uses more complex sentences

33 months

enough to tell others when she needs to go to the toilet.

Your child's language skills will also be improving. She will generally be asking as well as responding to a variety of simple questions and she is starting to use longer sentences of five or six words. She will mostly be understood by family members when she speaks, although strangers may have more difficulty in discerning her words. She will be starting to name some colours and may even have begun to count – or at least to repeat the words, even if she does not yet fully understand the concept of numbers properly at this point.

The activities in this chapter are ideal for engaging your child at this age, and you, too, should enjoy the fun of the energetic games here that are best played together, such as Dancing to music and Skittle alley. Many of the activities in this chapter and the final chapter are best played with a group of children of three or more – especially games such as the Island game – and they will encourage your child to interact with other children (though don't expect a huge amount of sharing at this stage). The outdoor games in the final chapter will ensure that your child is exposed to a rich variety of external influences and help her interact with the natural world around her.

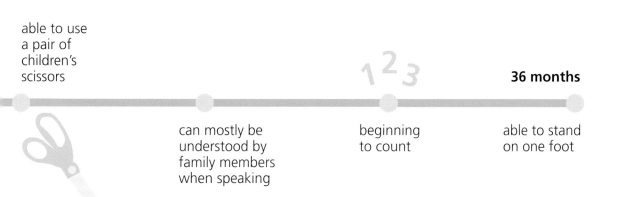

able to use
a pair of
children's
scissors

1 2 3   **36 months**

can mostly be
understood by
family members
when speaking

beginning
to count

able to stand
on one foot

The kitchen band

Open up your kitchen cupboards and you will find that your pots, pans, lids and wooden spoons can serve as excellent makeshift musical instruments. Your child will delight to hear the sounds they can produce when hitting each surface. This activity works well with one child or with many.

You will need

- Selection of pots and pans including at least 2 lids
- Wooden spoons
- Soft cloth
- Metal spoons
- Sheet of greaseproof paper
- Jar of dried beans

1 Set out the objects to be used as musical instruments. Show the children how the 'instruments' can be used.

2 The wooden spoon can be used to hit the top of the saucepans, like a drum.

3 The two lids can act as cymbals.

4 The soft cloth can be wrapped around one of the wooden spoons. This wrapped spoon will produce a softer sound when striking a saucepan lid.

5 The cupped parts of the two metal spoons can be hit together to make a noise.

6 The greaseproof paper can be folded and used to make a noise by pressing your lips against it and blowing.

7 The jar of dried beans can be held and shaken.

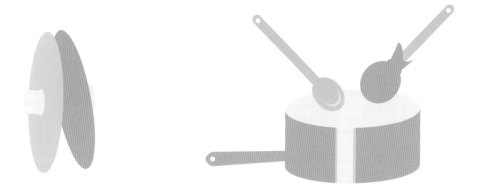

Dancing to music

Children love nothing better than dancing to music. They enjoy being able to express themselves through the music – and their pleasure is extended if more than one child joins in. For parents, nothing could be simpler than just providing the music, with the knowledge that your child is having so much fun and pleasure, and at the same time getting some exercise.

Dancing with scarves

1 Show your child the scarf and demonstrate how it can be waved in

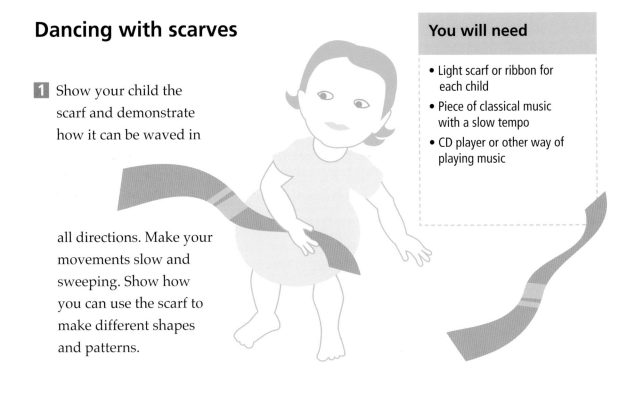

all directions. Make your movements slow and sweeping. Show how you can use the scarf to make different shapes and patterns.

You will need

- Light scarf or ribbon for each child
- Piece of classical music with a slow tempo
- CD player or other way of playing music

2 Let your child have a go at waving the scarf.

3 Put on the music and move together to it. Encourage your child to move lightly on her toes, while remembering to keep waving her scarf.

Dancing to different tempos

1 Put on the music and encourage your child to listen to the different tempos.

2 Together move to the music.

3 Encourage her to think not only about moving in time to the different speeds, but also how the movement changes. Use lighter movements for the faster sections, heavier movements for the slower sections.

4 When she is confident with changing the speed of her movement to match the music, encourage her to think about the different directions she can move in: backwards, forwards, turning and zigzag, all of which you should demonstrate first.

Other activities to try

Once she has mastered the movement with one scarf, give your child a second scarf.

- -

When she is confident in her movements, encourage your child to try them at different heights: up high and down low.

You will need

- Piece of music that changes tempo, such as *The Carnival of Animals* by Camille Saint-Saëns, or *Morning In the Hall of the Mountain King* by Edvard Grieg from the play *Peer Gynt*

Dances with stories

1 Begin by telling or reading the story to your child.

2 Listen to the music.

3 Work through the different stages of the story with your child, devising clear, simple movements that match the story.

4 You may need to recap certain stages of the story as she moves.

You will need

- Music with stories, such as *The Ugly Duckling* by Hans Christian Andersen, (music by Frank Loesser), *The Three Little Fishies* by Saxie Dowell or *Peter and the Wolf* by Sergei Prokofiev
- CD player or other way of playing music

Other activity to try

You could also find some appropriate music to go with your child's favourite story. Many children love dancing the story of *The Very Hungry Caterpillar* by Eric Carle.

Tip box ■ Let your child contribute as much as possible when deciding on the movements to match the story.

Dancing to a theme

1 Let your child listen to the music first. See if she can work out the different types of weather that might be expressed throughout the piece of music.

2 Show how a dance can tell a story to match the music. For example, start with a fine day, then put up your imaginary umbrella as rain begins to falls. You might jump over puddles and finally run to avoid a storm.

3 Let your child try the action to the music.

4 Move together around the room to the music.

5 Vary the music to introduce different themes, such as skating to music. Again let your child listen to the music first to get the 'feel' of it.

6 Demonstrate a skating action with swinging pendulum arms and long sliding steps.

7 Let your child try the action, and then move around the room together.

8 Once she is confident with the basic movement, introduce different directions and turns.

You will need

- Music with a theme, such as Beethoven's *Pastoral Symphony* (weather), or a piece of music with a strong, slow beat, such as *The Skater's Waltz* by Emile Waldteufel
- CD player or other way of playing music

The island game

Children love games that involve finding a safe place or base. In this game, the safe place is represented by a newspaper island, which they must get to when the word 'shark' is called out. This game also has the advantage that it requires minimal resources and preparation. It works best when you have a group of at least three children.

You will need

- Large indoor or outdoor space
- Old newspaper
- Scissors

1 If the newspaper is large (as in a broadsheet), cut each double sheet into two. If it is small (as in a tabloid), then there is no need to cut it.

2 Set out the pieces of paper over the area where the game is to be played, ensuring that there is enough space around each piece of paper so that children can run around it safely without bumping into each other or any obstacles in the room.

3 Explain to the children that the pieces of paper on the floor represent islands around which they must 'swim' until they hear the word 'shark', when they must jump onto an island.

4 Remind the children that they must move around the islands, not across them and to be aware of other children as they play the game.

Other activity to try

You also could play a musical version of this game. The children should 'swim' around the islands while the music is playing. When it stops they must jump onto an island.

Tip box

■ You could use hoops instead of newspaper to make the islands.

■ Older children would also enjoy joining in this game.

Fruit salad

This is a very simple game that children really respond to. It's a great way for children to burn off excess energy when they need to get active or have spent a while focusing on fine motor-skill activities. You will need a group of three or more children to play the game.

1 Ask the children to come into the centre of your designated space and tell them that they are going to play the game Fruit salad.

2 Point to each of the four corners of the space and give each corner the name of a fruit. For example, saying 'This is the strawberry corner', 'This is the apple corner', and so on.

3 Explain to the children that when you call out the name of a fruit, they all have to run to that corner.

4 Also let them know that when you call out 'Fruit salad', they need to run to the centre of the space.

You will need

- Large indoor or outdoor space
- Photocopy of the fruit template (see page 157)

Tip box ■ You might want to use coloured cones or markers to mark each corner as a different fruit, so that the children don't forget which corner represents which fruit.

5 Repeat the fruity names of the corners again. Then just point to each corner and ask the children to tell you the name, so you can make sure they all know which corner is which.

6 Start the game by calling out the first fruit of your choice. Give the children enough time to get to the corner before calling out the next fruit, and repeat until everyone is tired of the game!

Other activities to try

You don't have to stick with names of fruits. You could use colours and call the centre of the space the 'rainbow'.

If the children are getting breathless from running, or you want to vary the game, you could call out different actions, such as, 'Walk backwards to the banana corner'.

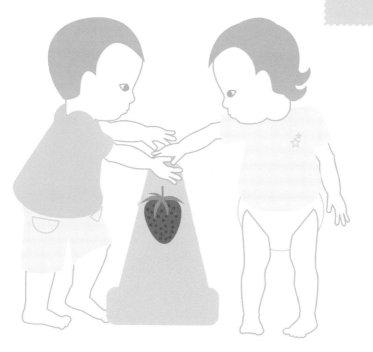

Skittle alley

Your child can have her own skittle alley in your home with this very easy-to-prepare skittle game. She will enjoy seeing the skittles tumble as he hits them with a rolling ball. This game can be played individually, in pairs or in teams. It's also a great game for focusing the mind and improving hand-eye co-ordination.

You will need

- Long narrow indoor or outdoor space, about 4 x 1 m (13 x 3 ft)
- 5 large empty water or soft-drink bottles with lids
- Lightweight medium-sized ball

Tip box

■ You could decorate the skittles with coloured stickers or number the skittles with a marker pen.

■ If the skittles seem a little unstable, you could fill them with a little water or with rice to weigh them down.

1. Set up all of the skittles in a row at one end of your chosen space.

2. Ask your child to stand at the other end of the space.

3. You could line cushions down the sides of the 'alley' to clearly define the path along which the ball rolls.

4. Demonstrate to her how to roll the ball to try to knock down the skittles.

5. Take turns trying to knock down the skittles and helping set them up again for the next player.

Other activity to try

Once your child becomes more confident with this game and is able to knock down more of the skittles, you could change the formation to make it more challenging for her.

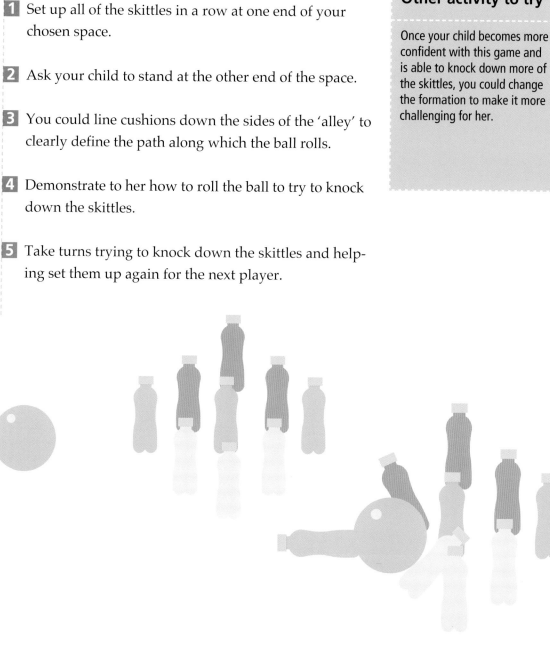

If you're happy and you know it . . .

This is a favourite action song that children love to sing. It's a real expression of joy and reminds them of all the actions of which they are capable. Since it involves the entire body, it's an engrossing way to demonstrate mindfulness.

If you're happy and you know it clap your
  hands. [Clap, clap]
If you're happy and you know it clap your
  hands. [Clap, clap]
If you're happy and you know it
  and you really want to show it . . .
If you're happy and you know it clap your
  hands. [Clap, clap]

If you're happy and you know it stamp
  your feet. [Stamp, stamp]
If you're happy and you know it stamp
  your feet. [Stamp, stamp]
If you're happy and you know it
  and you really want to show it . . .
If you're happy and you know it stamp
  your feet. [Stamp, stamp]

Continue the verses with other actions, such as:

• Jump up and down.
• Turn around.
• Stretch up high.
• March on the spot.
• Show a smile.

Traditionally the song always ends with the following verse:

If you're happy and you know it shout,
  'We are!' ['We are!']
If you're happy and you know it shout,
  'We are!' ['We are!']
If you're happy and you know it
and you really want to show it . . .
If you're happy and you know it shout,
  'We are!' ['We are!']

Try using the tune of the song to help your child to learn about the different parts of the body. You can do the actions of the song first, then ask your child to copy you.

Put your finger on your finger on your finger.
Put your finger on your finger on your finger.
Put your finger on your nose.
Turn around and touch your toes.
Put your finger on your finger on your finger.

Put your finger on your head on your head.
Put your finger on your head on your head.
Put your finger on your nose.
Turn around and touch your toes.
Put your finger on your head on your head.

Continue going through different body parts, repeating the nose and toes section. You might start at the head and work your way down the body.

Traffic lights game

From an early age children are very much drawn to the changing colours and patterns of traffic lights. This game is fun to play but it also reinforces the meaning of each traffic-light signal. Again, it's a stress-free game because no resources are required, you just need at least three children.

1 Ask the children to find a space.

2 Tell them they are going to play the Traffic lights game.

3 Remind them of what each colour represents. Red = Stop. Amber = Get ready to stop or get ready to go. Green = Go.

4 Tell the children that the traffic lights are currently on red, so they should be still.

5 Tell them that the lights have turned to amber so they should get ready to go.

You will need

• Large indoor or outdoor space

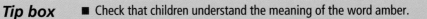

Tip box ■ Check that children understand the meaning of the word amber.

6 Tell them that the lights have now turned green, so they should go.

7 When they are new to the game, start them off just walking forwards when you say green. To make the game more challenging for older children, once they are confident of your instructions on each colour, choose a different action for the colours, such as walking on their tiptoes, taking giant steps or running in zigzags.

8 Go back to amber to get them to slow down, and then to red to stop.

9 Go through the sequence again and again with different actions on the green-light signal.

Other activity to try

There are endless action possibilities for this game. You could use animal actions, such as 'walk like a penguin', or transport actions, such as 'ride a bike'.

The animal game

Children are fascinated by animals and the different movements and sounds they make, and this game allows them to explore these. It is simple to play and it doesn't require any props. This is an excellent activity as a follow-up from a trip to a zoo or a farm.

1 Tell your child she is going to play the Animal game, and she has to act like the animal you show her.

2 Animal picture cards or toy models are a fun accessory to this game, but they are not necessary to play. If you are using them, pick one up and show it to your child. If not, you can just tell her the name of an animal. Make sure you only choose animals that she will be familiar with, especially for younger children.

3 Ask your child to show you what noise that animal makes. If she has any trouble with this at first, make the noise yourself and ask her to copy you.

4 Ask her to pretend she is that animal and move around the room. Again, if she has trouble doing this, you can get her started. For example, as an elephant you might use one of your arms to swing like a trunk, or for a penguin, put your feet together and waddle forwards.

You will need

- Picture cards of a variety of animals, or a selection of animal toys (optional)

Other activity to try

You could also play a 'who am I?' version of this game. Make the movements and the sounds of an animal and ask your child to guess what animal you are.

Letting go meditation

When things get too much as a parent and you feel assaulted by difficult emotions, such as anger, frustration or guilt, it can be helpful to take a step back – this mindful activity is the first stage in letting go of unhelpful feelings.

1 First, look at the effects this emotion is having on your body. Is your breathing more rapid? Are your fists clenched? Are you holding your breath? You don't have to do anything about this; don't feel guilty or judge these emotions, just note their physical effects.

2 Now let go of any effort to do anything. Sit and close your eyes. Don't analyse or try to change anything. Let go of any sense of responsibility. Just surrender.

3 As you inhale, say the word 'Let' to yourself. As you exhale say the word 'Go' in your head. Repeat the words a few times.

4 Finally, focus attention on your heart. As you inhale, feel your ribs expand and your chest broaden. Keep the sense of lift in your breastbone as you exhale. Repeat a few times. Submit to the love and peace in your heart and trust that they will support you.

Language and stories

It is important to show children not only the sheer pleasure that can be afforded by language but also how it can be used as a powerful tool to express their feelings and emotions. As parents you should take every opportunity to enrich your child's life with stories, poetry and songs. The activities in this chapter encompass every aspect of language development from clapping rhythm games to using their imagination to create stories.

Mindful timeline: 3+ years

Once he reaches three years old, your child will have an ever-increasing roster of friends. The more time he spends with them the more he will learn about co-operation and playing together. In play he will learn that the ability to share with others is important. If your child has siblings then he may have already had some experience of sharing or being asked to share, but if he is an only child it will be new to him and he may find it difficult to start with. Coupled with this there will inevitably be conflict, and he will also learn how to negotiate, whether it's with his friends for another turn with the bricks or with his parents for an extra biscuit.

Your child's sense of independence will now have been augmented by his increasing ability to dress and undress himself with simple items of clothing, although some parental input into his exact choices of clothes may still be required to avoid unseasonal whims. He will now also be able to put his shoes on by himself, but

Timeline

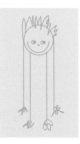

co-operates more
with other children

increasingly able
to share

36 months

able to draw
recognisable
shapes

if the shoes have laces they will have to be tied by someone else.

By this time, your child will be starting to have a better understanding of himself and his surroundings. As a result he will be able to understand the difference between himself and younger children, but as yet unable to comprehend the difference between himself and older children. He will be able to say his age and will feel quite grown up by now, so he will take great pleasure in looking at photos of himself as a baby.

The activities in this chapter will help to develop your child's ever-increasing vocabulary as well as encouraging an interest in stories. You will also be able to prompt your child's memory of words, stories and objects with activities like I went to the shop and bought . . . and Set stories with props, where he will begin to associate key objects and props with the stories he knows. Encouraging him to participate in activities such as Making up stories will also develop his enthusiasm for making up and sharing his own stories with you.

capable of
dressing and
undressing self

increasingly
independent

capable of
putting on
shoes

My family and friends

Family and friends are very important to young children, not only in the social sense but also as a means of identifying themselves and their place in the world. This next activity will help your child to establish who his family members are and where they fit in, in relation to him.

1 Set out the photographs of just the immediate family, scissors, pencil and marker pen.

2 Invite your child to come and join you.

3 Explain to him that he is going to make a house with all the members of the family in it.

4 Let him select one of the photographs.

5 In pencil, mark a circle around the photograph so that it will fit in one of the windows of the house.

6 If he is able, let him trace around the pencil circle with the marker pen.

You will need

- Photographs of members of your family and of your extended family
- Pair of child's scissors
- Pencil
- Marker pen
- House template (see page 158), you may need more than one
- Glue stick
- Some crayons, pencil crayons, or felt-tip pens
- Large sheet of paper to stick the houses onto

Tip box ■ Remember to include photos of any pets you may have.

■ This could be an ongoing project done over a period of a week or two.

7 Start cutting around the circle and then, if he is able, let him complete it.

8 Repeat steps 4 to 7 with another photograph until all the immediate family photographs have been cut out.

9 Take the photocopy of the house and let your child select one of the photographs.

10 Explain to him that he needs to choose which window he would like to stick the photograph in.

11 Once selected, he needs to glue the back of the photo and stick it in the window.

12 Repeat the process until all the photographs have been stuck onto the house.

13 Under each window write the name of the family member in the photograph.

14 Invite your child to colour in the picture.

15 Take another photocopy of the house and repeat the above steps but this time use photographs of any grandparents.

16 The same can be done on a separate house for any other extended family members like aunts, uncles, cousins and so on.

17 When all the houses are complete you may like to stick them onto a large sheet of paper, with the immediate family house in the centre and all the other houses around it.

18 Draw a connecting line with an arrow from an immediate family member to the related extended family member's house. On the line write, for example, 'Grandma and Grandpa's house, we get there by car'. As well as the word 'car' draw a picture of a car.

19 Continue until all the family members' houses have been connected up.

20 At the top of the sheet of paper you may like to write 'All my family'.

Other activities to try

After having completed all your family you could repeat the same activity, but this time your child could make separate houses to include all his friends.

Draw an extra window if there are not enough, or you could create a garden around the house and put other family members there.

The clapping game

This fun game requires no resources, just a pair of hands. It can be played with one child or as many children as you wish. While your child is having fun, subconsciously he is developing an awareness of the rhythms and patterns of speech.

1 Sit facing your child, or if there is more than one child, in a circle.

2 Start by saying the child's name out loud and as you do so, clap out the name according to the number of syllables. If there is more than one child, go through their names as well.

3 Clap out the names of family and friends.

4 Clap out their favourite animals or things your child likes to eat.

Tip box ■ Instead of hands, you could use homemade instruments. See the Kitchen Band on page 100.

I went to the shop and bought . . .

3¹/₂+ years

You may have played the game as a child where you have to remember a cumulative list of items bought on a supposed shopping trip. This is a simpler version for younger children. It's best played with two or more children.

1 Ask the children to sit in a circle.

2 Tell them that they are going to play a game called I went to the shop and bought . . .

3 Put the objects in the centre of the circle.

4 Give the basket to the youngest child.

5 Let him choose an object from the selection.

6 When he has chosen, ask him to say, 'I went to the shop and bought . . .' followed by the name of the object they selected. Then he puts the object in the basket.

You will need

- Selection of child-friendly objects (each child should have 1 object to put in the basket)
- Medium-to-large basket
- Tea towel or cloth large enough to cover the basket

Tip box   ■ If a child is having difficulty remembering, give him some hints, but stress to the other children not to give the answer away.

Other activity to try

As the children gain more confidence in remembering, you can increase the number of objects each child selects to put in the basket.

7 The basket is passed around to the next child, who selects another object to put in the basket.

8 When all the objects have been put in, cover the basket with the tea towel.

9 Ask each child in turn if they can remember what object they bought.

10 When all the children have been asked, uncover the basket so the children can see if they were correct.

Alphabet hunt

This is another version of hide and seek, only instead of children hiding, it is done with objects. Each object should have the same initial letter sound, so that your child becomes more familiar with the alphabet and the way the letters sound.

You will need

- 4 medium-to-small objects, each with the same initial letter sound e.g. carrot, comb and clip

1 Show the objects to your child.

2 Check with your child that he is clear as to what the objects are.

3 Tell him that you are going to hide the objects.

4 Ask him to cover his eyes while you hide the objects.

5 Tell him when you are ready and then ask him to find the objects.

6 If he is having difficulty finding one of the objects, you might need to give him a clue.

7 The game is over when all the objects have been found.

8 Recap the objects that have been found and the letter that they all start with.

Other activity to try

Once your child is confident finding the objects, you could increase the number of objects to be found.

When this game has been mastered, and as your child becomes more familiar with letters, instead of finding objects that all begin with the same letter, try going through the whole alphabet. Ask your child to find an object that begins with the letter 'a', then the letter 'b', and so on. Don't go through the whole alphabet at once; try four letters one day, and perhaps the next four letters the following day.

Tip box ■ If you are playing this with more than one child, ensure that there is one object for each child. Ask each child which object they would like to look for. Once they have found their object they could help another child if needed.

Making up stories

In this game a prop acts as the starting point for a story of your child's own making. You could use literally anything, but listed below are some suggestions that work particularly well.

1 Tell your child he is going to make up a story.

2 Show him the prop that you have chosen for him.

3 For the adult shoes, you might like to suggest that they belong to a giant. Ask your child to describe the giant, where he or she lives and what adventure does he/she go on.

You will need

- Selection of props such as a pair of adult shoes, a selection of hats or a wrapped-up parcel with a sign saying 'please open me' – inside there should be an object of your choice

---

Tip box

■ Children will need continuous prompting to help them develop the story. Ask questions such as: What happened next? Did they get back safely? Was he scared when he saw the lion?

■ You will need to act as a guide to bring the story to an end.

4 For the selection of hats, you might explain to your child that she is going to pretend that the hats belong to some other people. Ask him to describe them and why they wear the hats.

5 Children can't resist the appeal of unwrapping a parcel, so this one makes a great starting point for a story. Whatever you put in the parcel is going to determine the type of story you create. You might put a ring in the parcel, for example, and explain that the ring has special powers and then ask your child to tell you what they might be and who owns the ring.

Set stories with props

In this game you are using the props to tell a story with which the child or children are already familiar. They have to guess from the props set out before them which story it is, tell that story and then act it out. Think of a favourite story and what props you could use to represent the story that your child will instantly recognise and associate with it.

You will need

Props appropriate to the story – for example, for Goldilocks and the Three Bears:

- Large, medium and small bowls
- 3 spoons
- Box of porridge oats

1 Lay out all of the props you have chosen in front of your child.

2 Ask him what story he knows that includes three bowls of porridge. You might need to point out the different sizes of the bowls to help him.

3 You could then ask why the story is called 'Goldilocks and the Three Bears'. What does this little girl do?

4 Keep asking questions until your child has told all the main events in the story.

5 Get your child to use the props to mime out the events of the story.

Other activity to try

You can play this activity with any number of children's stories. For example, for Little Red Riding Hood you would need props such as a red cape with a hood, or just a red hooded jumper would work well, and a basket of goodies for her to take to Grandma. Ask your child what story includes a red cape. You could then ask why the story is called Little Red Riding Hood, what does this little girl do? Again, keep asking questions until he has told all the main events in the story.

Tip box   ■ If you are doing this with several children, make sure you have chosen a story each of the children is familiar with.

Out and about

For a child, every day is a day of discovery and of learning. This does not mean that as a parent you have to bombard your child with new experiences. Children derive the utmost pleasure from observing the tiniest insect or hearing leaves being rustled by the wind. The key to helping your child discover the joy of the world around them is to allow them time to explore, investigate and question. The activities in this final chapter will stimulate and engage your child's natural curiosity and expand their awareness of the world they live in.

Sticky the Squirrel

This is a great game as it combines so many activities and skills. It begins with the character of Sticky the squirrel. In a story about him your child will learn about squirrels and their habitat. The game ends with a mindful seek-and-find activity.

Before you start the story you will need to cut out the template of Sticky, letting your child help you if she is able. Then ask your child to colour in the picture and write at the top of the sheet 'Sticky the Squirrel'. Then you're ready to tell the story of how Stanley the Squirrel became sticky.

You will need

- Photocopy of the squirrel template (see page 159)
- Child's scissors
- Adult scissors
- Coloured pencils, crayons or felt-tip pens
- Garden or park
- Double-sided tape
- Assortment of natural objects such as leaves or twigs

How Stanley the Squirrel became Sticky

Once there was a squirrel called Stanley. He was a very inquisitive squirrel, who liked to go exploring all through the woods where he lived. Up high in the treetops, down in deep hollows under piles of autumn leaves, there was no place that Stanley had not explored. One day on the soft breeze came a delicious, sweet smell. Stanley followed the smell and it led him to a beehive. The delicious smell was, of course, honey. Now Stanley knew that bees sting, so he waited until the bees had flown away to collect some nectar. Then he raced into the hive to steal some of the delicious honeycomb. Away he ran with it, taking it to his favourite tree. Unfortunately Stanley was not a very tidy eater; in fact he was rather messy. The more honey he ate, the more it spread all over his fur, from the top of his head to the tip of his tail. Try as he might he could not remove the honey from his fur. Everywhere he went all sorts of things stuck to him: leaves, twigs and feathers. So since that day Stanley became known as Sticky.

Tip box
- Let your child make their own selection of items to stick on but remind her that they need to be small and light.
- Check that the outdoor area is free from prickly plants or any sharp objects, etc.
- This is a good opportunity to explain not to pick living things such as plants.
- If more than one child is playing the game, ensure you make a photocopy for each child.

1. Take the drawing of the squirrel to your outside space.

2. Ask your child to rub her hand over the drawing. Explain that at the moment he's Stanley the squirrel, but that you are going to turn him into Sticky the squirrel.

3. Cut small pieces of double-sided tape and stick them onto the squirrel.

4. Peel off the top protective pieces and let your child feel a piece so she can see that Stanley is now Sticky.

5. Ask her to collect and stick on any objects that she thinks may have stuck to Sticky.

Other activity to try

If you don't have squirrels where you live, choose an animal that does inhabit your local area. You will have to draw your own picture of the animal for your child to use.

I spy

I doubt there is any parent who has not played this game, and it continues to be a favourite with children of all ages. When you introduce the game, say 'Let's put on our looking eyes', and mime circles around your eyes with your fingers. This helps a child focus, and we can learn from it as parents, too, by putting on imaginary glasses whenever we want to feel more focused!

1 If your child is new to the game, you could start by placing a group of objects on a tray. The 'spied' object must come from one of the objects on the tray. When your child understands the objective of the game, place these objects around the room.

2 Once the game has been understood in this way, introduce the standard way of playing 'I Spy'. You will need to go first.

3 Explain that you are now 'spying' something from the room. Spy something very easy to start with.

4 If your child is having difficulty guessing what it is, give some clues – the shape, the size, what it's made from and so on.

Colours in nature

Whatever the environment, children are drawn to colour. This seek-and-find game introduces your child to the huge variety of colours to be found in nature, and increases your appreciation of natural beauty, too. It aids visual discrimination and colour-matching skills.

1 Start by gluing your coloured squares onto the cardboard in two rows of three, evenly spaced across the cardboard.

2 Next to each coloured square put a piece of double-sided tape of a similar width to the square. At this stage do not peel off the tape's top protective strip.

3 Take the card with you to your outdoor play area and explain to your child that she is going to play a game of colour-matching.

You will need

- Glue stick
- 6 coloured squares of paper approximately 4 x 4 cm (1½ x 1½ in) in a variety of colours to match your outdoor space (such as browns, reds, oranges, greens)
- Cardboard or stiff paper approximately 30 x 20 cm (12 x 8 in)
- Double-sided tape
- Scissors
- Outdoor space

Tip box

■ Emphasise and repeat the name of the colour when your child is looking for an object of that colour: 'You need to find something red'.

■ You might want to begin by finding three colours and then work up to six.

4 Focus in on one colour and ask her to find that colour in the plants or trees around her. Explain that it just needs to be a very small amount of that colour so she can stick it on to the cardboard.

5 Give her the cardboard and help her look for the first colour. Start by deliberately choosing colours that don't match. Put the object next to the square of paper and say, 'It's not the same'. In this way, she will come to understand that she needs to find an object the same colour as the square.

6 When she finds an object, show her how to peel off the top strip of the double-sided tape and stick the object to the tape.

7 When all the colours have been matched, let her know what a good job she has done in finding and matching the colours. Run through all the things you found and their colours, for example, 'We found a red leaf'.

Other activities to try

As she gets more confident in finding, let your child explore by herself and show you her finds.

Repeat the game, making a new colour board with colours to reflect the changing seasons.

Textures in nature

This is a seek-and-find game that gets you both walking outdoors together and helps you and your child to tune into your sense of touch as you explore the huge variety of textures to be found in the outdoor world. The game starts with you choosing a range of natural objects to delight your child.

You will need

- Garden or park
- Collection of natural objects with varied textures that your child can clearly distinguish between
- Small container

1. Begin by collecting a small range of objects from the garden or park – such as leaves, small stones, bark, twigs, feathers, petals and grasses. Put them in the container. Don't let your child help for now, so it's more of a surprise when he has to do the seeking.

2. Let your child select one of the objects in the container.

3. Tell her that she needs to find where in the garden or park it came from.

4. Walk around the garden together, comparing the texture of the object in your child's hand with the tree bark, the grass and so on, so she gets the idea that she needs to match up the object using her sense of touch.

5. When you find the correct match, let her place the object in her hand with the matching one.

6. Once you've matched everything in the container, let your child do the hunting and you do the seeking.

Other activity to try

The beach is a fun place to explore texture – from the different feel of sand and shingle to the many types of rock and shell.

Tip box

■ Start with three objects, working up to six when the game is repeated.

■ Make sure that the matching object is accessible, and if not, cheat a bit and place it so that your child can get at it.

Nature collage

Children love to create, and this activity allows them to freely create a collage using the natural resources of whatever is to hand in an outdoor space. This activity is best suited to autumn when there will be a greater variety of colours in the grasses, leaves, nuts and seeds available. For parents, the activity encourages awareness of the passing of time and of impermanence.

1 Find a level piece of ground on which to make the collage. It can be as big or small as you wish.

2 Say to your child that she is going to make a collage using all the natural things around her.

3 Ask her to begin by collecting everything she thinks would look good in her collage.

4 Make a little pile of everything that has been collected next to where the collage is to be created.

You will need

- Outdoor space with a good variety of natural objects, such as leaves, twigs, bark, nuts and seeds (there is no need for glue, as this is a natural rather than a permanent collage)

Tip box

■ You might want to work alongside your child, creating your own collage, as this will help her to get some ideas.

■ Check the area for prickly plants and point them out to your child.
■ Remind her that things such as berries are only for the birds.

5 When enough things have been collected, ask her to see if she can make a picture or pattern with them. Suggest different shapes or patterns, like circles, spirals or zigzags.

6 Once the collage is complete, allow her to step back and admire her creation.

Other activity to try

When your child has completed this, you could collect up some of the objects she has used to take home, so that she can make a smaller scale collage on paper as well.

Treasure trail

Children love following a trail, especially if they know there will be treasure at the end. This game can be played with as many or as few children as you wish. It's also a great game for older siblings to join in with. Don't worry about reluctant walkers; they will be so busy having fun following the trail they won't even realise how active they are being.

1 Choose your outdoor space. You could play in a large garden, a park, bushland or woodland – whatever is available nearby.

2 Set a trail using the chalk to mark the way with large arrows, or blobs of flour when there isn't a place for an arrow.

3 Your trail should take about 30 minutes' walking time.

You will need

- Outdoor space
- Piece of chalk
- Small bag of flour
- Treasure (such as stickers, biscuits, chocolate coins)

Tip box

- When following the trail, don't let the children race too far ahead of you. Always keep them within your sight.
- If you are in a large group, have short rest stops to allow everyone to catch up and also ensure everyone stays together.
- Make sure all your chalk arrows and blobs of flour are clearly visible at a child's sight level.

4 Explain to the children that they are going to follow a trail and that they need to look out for white arrows and blobs of flour.

5 When they get to the end of the trail, reward them with their treasure. This could be anything from a special sticker to their favourite biscuit or you could even hide some chocolate coins.

Seek and find

This is a great game to play when you are outside and have no resources to hand. It works best when played with several children. Children love the competitive element of trying to find items before anyone else. This game also has the advantage that within a group it can be played individually, in pairs or, if you have a lot of children, in teams.

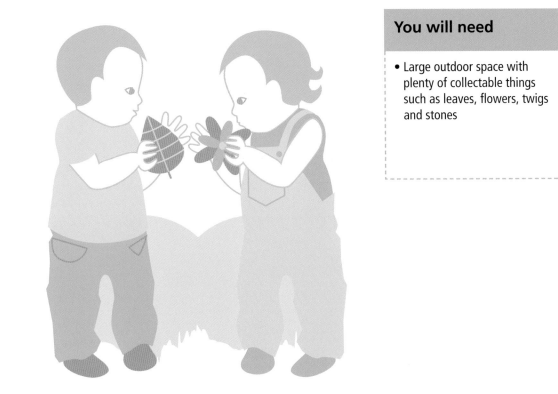

You will need

- Large outdoor space with plenty of collectable things such as leaves, flowers, twigs and stones

1 Decide what objects you are going to ask the children to collect. For example, three green leaves, two twigs, one feather.

2 Tell the children what they have to find.

3 Send the children off to start hunting.

4 When they start returning with some of their finds, make a separate pile for each child.

5 When they have found all their collectables, ask them to sit next to their pile.

6 The game is over when all children have completed the task.

Other activity to try

As children become more familiar with these natural objects, you can start to make the game more challenging by asking them to find more specific items. Instead of asking them to find a flower, for example, ask them to find a daisy (only choose simple flowers they are familiar with, and that you can see are growing in an obvious place).

Tip box

■ For younger children, just give them one item to find at any one time. Once the children return with the object, tell them the next one on the list. Don't ask them to find more than one or two items.

■ Give each child as much freedom as possible in finding things for themselves, although you might need to step in to help now and then.

Make a sandcastle

The charm of the sandpit is indisputable. It's also a perfect forum for your child to engage with natural materials creatively on a large scale. They will be entranced by the texture and qualities of the sand, and be encouraged to stretch their powers of co-ordination and building skills.

You will need

- Sandpit or box, or a trip to the seaside
- Suitable scoop or spade
- Trays, moulds or buckets
- Water
- Decorative objects (such as shells, leaves, pebbles, flags)

1 Sit with your child and explore the possibilities of the sand by scooping, patting and digging.

2 As she gets bolder, show your child how to fill a mould or bucket and let her try it herself.

3 Turn the containers out to form shapes in the sand. Try mixing with water to get a firmer mould and create new textures for her to play with.

4 Show your child how to start building walls to connect together all the mounds she has made and complete her castle.

5 You can decorate the finished result with any objects you can find, such as shells, leaves, pebbles or even a small flag to plant in one of the castle's towers.

Other activity to try

When your castle is complete, you and your child can build a moat around the outside of it. With the wet sand, show her how she can build a bridge across the water.

| *Tip box* | ■ Beware of sand in the eyes, ears and mouth. Keep a bottle of clean water and a soft cloth handy in case of accidents.
 ■ If more than one child is playing, make sure no one starts throwing sand. | ■ If you're at the seaside, keep an eye on the tides and on how far your child is exploring. |

Picnic time

2+
years

Picnics are exciting for children and adults of all ages. Even just heading out into the garden can feel like an adventure and a break from routine. Involving your child in every stage of the picnic will expand her enjoyment and develop her ideas about how and where food can be consumed, what it looks and feels like in its different forms, and so on, introducing the basics of mindful eating.

1 Preparation is half the fun. Tell your child you will be going on a picnic and let her help you prepare it. Pack the picnic together, talking about the different foods and where you'll be eating them.

2 Find a place outside that is quiet and safe to have your picnic. It doesn't have to be an adventurous setting, the back garden is fine.

3 Spread out your blanket and make sure you and your child are well protected from the sun, if needed.

4 Lay out the food by group and get your child to move around and have some of each. For each food type, talk

You will need

- Blanket
- Sunshade, if necessary
- Picnic food, to include all the food groups, e.g. pasta, fruit, eggs, yogurt, vegetables, chocolate
- Drinks

Tip box   ■ You can combine your picnic with any number of the other outdoor activities suggested in this chapter.

about the colours, shapes and flavours she can see, feel and taste. The point is to savour the sensory pleasures of the food, and the enhanced smells and flavours that come from being outside.

5 Sing along with your child to the song 'The Teddy Bear's Picnic'. This is a good song to sing while you're preparing the picnic, to keep her interested, and when you're outside enjoying your picnic together. You could even take some of her teddy bears out on the picnic with you.

If you go down to the woods today
You're sure of a big surprise.
If you go down to the woods today
You'd better go in disguise.
For every bear that ever there was
Will gather there for certain, because
Today's the day the Teddy Bears
*   have their picnic.*

Street spy

This walking with awareness technique has the advantage of encouraging your child to walk that bit faster – invaluable if you need to get home in a hurry. You might try it yourself whenever your find yourself dawdling or any time you want to still racing thoughts. The idea is to ask your child to spy specific things while you are out and about. The possibilities are endless, which means you can adapt the activity to the age of your child. Here are some suggestions to get you started.

1 Ask your child to guess what colour the front door of the next house will be.

2 Ask her to find a door that is the same colour as your own front door.

3 Ask her to find a car with a number plate containing the first letter in her name.

4 Ask her to count the number of red cars she can see.

Tip box ■ Always keep your child on the inside of you when walking down the street, especially when playing this game, when your child's attention will be taken with objects rather than potential oncoming traffic.

Nature meditation

We don't have to go outdoors to commune with nature – as living beings we are nature, as natural as the trees and grass in the park. This visualisation helps you become more mindful of that.

1 Lie on your back with your knees bent and your feet flat on the ground. Rest your arms a little way from your sides, palms upwards. Close your eyes.

2 Think about the ground beneath you – the floor made of wood or stone and the earth beneath that. Think of the firm, grounding qualities of wood, stone and earth.

3 Now imagine you are lying in a forest on the same earth, but surrounded by trees growing towards the sun, looking up into a canopy of leaves. What can you hear? What can you smell?

4 After a while, come back to the sense of yourself lying in your own surroundings, but be aware that you too are part of nature. You only have to look inside to appreciate this connection to the big wide world.

Template 1

Story gloves

Cut out the figures to tell the story of *Goldilocks and the Three Bears*

Template 2

Fruit salad

Template 3

My family and friends

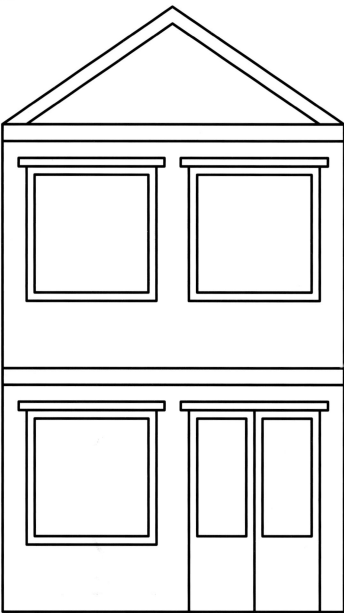

Template 4

Sticky the Squirrel

Index